What's Age Got to Do with It?

Essays by Dr. Shirley Zussman

Dedication

To all the people who have contributed to make my life the wonderful
journey it has been for all these years.

Foreword

No birthday celebration, wedding, engagement party or graduation ever goes by that Shirley (Marc's and Carol's mother) forgets to write a poem to the honored guest. At her 90th birthday party, at every person's place was a poem she had written about that person.

Shirley is a writer through and through. Now, at 103 years of age, the highlight of her week is her neighborhood writing group and preparing a new essay each week for that week's meeting. In 2008, Shirley started a blog called "What's Age Got to Do with It?" This book contains many of the essays from that blog in addition to some of her more recent pieces. The blog is found at szussman.blogspot.com, where Shirley explains, "We live in a culture obsessed with youth and beauty. At the same time people are living longer than in any other period in history and as people age they are healthier, more active and more imbued with a zest for life. So, what's age got to do with it??"

Almost all of her essays have been written in her later '90s and early 100's. They portray a stimulating view of her personal reflections, family memories, the tech revolution, her work as a sex therapist and the experience of aging. Here, as very few people have been able to do, she shows that aging has nothing to do with creativity, energy, insight, love and living a full life.

Marc Zussman & Becky Turner, San Francisco

June 3, 2017

Acknowledgements

Five of the stories included were published previously in a 2016 book entitled *Five Minute Limit: An Anthology*. In addition, a story from both Glamour magazine and Time magazine are included. Cover photograph is from an article in the New York Post.

TABLE OF CONTENTS

Family Stories

Shirley (left) with her mother, father, and siblings (Spencer and Vera)

HOUSE ARREST

I grew up in my family's brownstone house on E. 10th St. opposite Tompkin's Square Park. It was really a yellow brick house and one of five adjacent houses known as Doctor's Row because all the owners were physicians as was my father. He had an office on the ground floor and we lived on the floor above. One night we were having dinner when the doorbell rang in what seemed a demanding way. My father said: "I'll get it, it's probably a patient who's come to the wrong floor". When he opened the door, there stood a policeman, a big tall man. I wasn't frightened because a policeman could need my father's help, too. But he spoke in a gruff voice and demanded that my father take him to the basement. Quietly, my father asked, "What is this about?" He didn't answer quietly but rather sounded like some of the bullies in my school. There was no more talk and he followed my father out of the door. My sister and I began to cry. My mother tried to sooth us. "Your father is a very wise man. He'll take care of the situation". I was still scared, but I was a little disappointed that my father could be bullied.

My mother cuddled us until my father returned alone. He was chuckling. Someone had reported that there was a dead man in our basement! "It's about that skeletal model that I brought home from Germany to teach anatomy to my medical students at the hospital". The janitor had come across it and spread the rumor that there was a dead body in our basement.

After he left us, we named the model Joe and the friendly policeman would ask us how Joe was doing and saw to it that those bullies never came near us again.

SPIN THE BOTTLE

When I was eight years old, I lived with my parents, my sister and brother in Berlin. It was an exciting life, seeing new sights and having amazing experiences. However, I do remember from those many, many years ago something that disturbed me very much and that I did not understand then, as I do now, as a cultural difference. My mother let other men kiss her, not on her lips or her check as my father kissed her, but on her hand. I watched as a male friend bent slightly from the waist, my mother extended her hand, and that hand, my mother's hand, was kissed, not only by one man, but a number of men on different occasions. I remember crying almost every time I witnessed this behavior. Little did I know then that people kiss in different ways in different places in the world. Kissing the back of the hand was a common sign of respect in Victorian England as well as all over Europe in genteel circles.

The Eskimos, Polynesians and Malaysians rub noses rather than kiss lips as a way of showing affection and sexual interest. By the way, the Eskimos call making love, laughing time. Among the Indian tribes, hand pressing was more a part of courtship custom than kissing. The Japanese male considered the nape of his partner's neck more erotic than her lips.

13

Even in our own society, until TV and the movies glamorized kissing and gave everyone permission to copy what they saw, kissing was not as common among the less educated segments of society, whereas the more educated spent more time kissing and less in explicit sexual activity. Times have changed this!

The different ways in which societies view kissing certainly demonstrates the way sexual behavior is shaped by culture. If I had known that those kisses planted on my mother's hand all those years ago were a sign of respect, rather than desire, my eight year old self would have been spared a lot of tears.

For those who enjoy the erotic pleasure of kissing someone they love on the lips, I say, "Vive la Difference".

THE MIRACLE WORKER

My father was a raconteur par excellence. He was able to make an extraordinary story out of an ordinary event. He loved telling his stories, loved the laughter that followed a laughter he shared, his whole body shaking in delight.

One of the stories that came to my mind recently, as thoughts of my father emerged across the holiday table, was of a visit he made to the home of one of his first patients.

He was a newly minted doctor, who had just opened an office on the Lower East Side of Manhattan. That area was very different then than the hip neighborhood it is today. Most of the people who lived there then were recent European immigrants, barely able to speak English. They lived in small tenement houses, with many occupants sharing limited space. Insurance and Medicare were words they had never heard.

Shortly after he opened his office, he was called to one of these tenement houses. The situation was described as an emergency – the head of the household was dying. A home visit was the order of the day.

There were no telephones, no cell phone, no papers. My father stood in front of the tenement and a member of the household leaned out of the window to direct him to a fourth floor apartment.

While he was climbing the stairs, he heard crying and moaning. When he arrived at the proper door, a weeping woman told him "Mein mann is gestorben" – he's dead! My father was led into the room where he saw a body on the bed, covered in newspaper. He extended his sympathy and was about to turn back, when the family beseeched him to stay while they ran around the streets, conveying the sad news to relatives and friends.

He agreed and sat down in a chair near a window, filling out some papers. After a few minutes, his eye fell on the bed nearby and he was started to notice that the newspaper covering the body was stirring. He concluded it was because of a breeze form the window. But there was no breeze – it was a hot, humid day.

After a few minutes, he saw more movement of the newspaper. He rushed over to the bed, tore off the paper and found that the man was indeed alive. What he did in those moments is not very clear in my memory; but when the family returned, he announced that their beloved relative was indeed alive and breathing, as they could all see for themselves.

The family was beside itself with joy. They embraced my father and ran into the street, proclaiming that the new, young doctor had brought a dead man to life! He was a miracle worker, a savior.

From that day on, the new young doctor became an overnight success. His bell rang all day and, yes, all night. His practice was so busy; he had to hire an assistant and his career was off to a blazing start.

OCCUPATIONAL HAZARD

A friend of mine recently returned from a long trip – it was a trip with a group organized by a travel company. My friend enjoyed the trip as a whole but described one problem he experienced. He is an orthopedist, which became known to the group. For the most part, the group was middle aged and frequently someone would ask my friend for advice about his various aches and pains. "What do you recommend would ease my pain? Am I taking the right pills?" My friend felt the question interfered with his leaving his work behind.

As he told me this, I was reminded about what became one of my father's favorite stories and mine as well.

He was an ear, nose and throat and specialist. On vacation, numerous people would describe that they had ringing in their ears, a scratchy throat, and other complaints quite common to a middle-aged population. My father said he couldn't enjoy his swim or his quiet time on the terrace – nor did he want to be rude. He felt harassed at times.

One year, before leaving for a vacation, he wondered how he

could avoid the constant barrage of complaints and the asking for advice.

Finally, he got it! When asked what he did for a living, he would say he was a <u>kosher butcher</u>. He never had any trouble again.

Tuesday, December 2, 2008

ON THE MARCH

This is a story about Joe, not Joe the plumber, who has already faded into obscurity, but Joe, my cousin. He was about 40 at the time of this story – single, a musician and a great favorite in the family. He played the piano at all our parties and never seemed to get tired at meeting requests for our favorite songs.

One day we heard that Joe had been taken to Mr. Sinai Hospital, suffering from stomach pains. My father decided to visit him there. When he entered Joe's hospital room, Grace, Joe's sister, was there, glad to see a member of the family.

As a physician, my father was permitted to read a patient's medical chart, which was attached to the bed, where Joe lay, pale and nervous in a hospital gown.

After reading the chart for some time, my father put it down and said to Joe in a gentle but firm voice –

"Joe, I want you to get dressed. You're leaving the hospital with me". Joe looked at my father with astonishment.

"Uncle Louis, I love you and respect you, but what are you

about?! My surgery is scheduled for the day after tomorrow. I have one of the best surgeons in the city and the chief of surgery here".

"Joe", my father responded, "If you don't get dressed, you're leaving in your hospital gown!"

And that is how the story goes... My father led the parade; Joe followed him in his gown and his sister after him, carrying a beautiful plant she had brought as a gift. As she told it later, "so it wouldn't be a total loss".

The three of them marched out of the hospital. No one noticed them; no one stopped them.

Shortly after, Joe moved to California. He got a job at MGM, a major Hollywood studio, as a musician. He lived in California until his death at the age of 81. He never had that abdominal surgery, nor did he suffer any abdominal pain after his march through Mt. Sinai Hospital in his hospital gown.

FEATHERING MY NEST

When I was a teenager, oh, so long ago, I began to have fantasies of a prince who would enter my life and soon we would go off and live together happily ever after! Soon the place where we would live became the major focus of the fantasy. It was never a cottage in the woods; it was never a mansion in a fashionable suburb. No, it was always similar to places in which I had lived with my family – a brownstone facing a park – a spacious city apartment.

The difference was that in the fantasy I could make all the decisions as to how our living quarters would be decorated – the colors, the furniture, and the art – how it would be arranged in the space my prince and I occupied.

It wasn't that I found my parents' décor distasteful, but I wanted to make the decisions; and in the fantasy, I could.

Now that I look back, older and wiser, what troubled me – and fed my fantasy, was that my mother often consulted my sister before making any decorating decisions – my sister had "the eye", the talent for design and composition; and indeed, in her adult life she became an interior decorator. To this day, in her 90s, she is frequently consulted about anything that involves "the eye".

Years passed. The prince and I found each other and we did go off together to set up our first home – to feather our nest. I must confess that I turned to my sister that first time for some guidance. After that I took the plunge and made my own decisions and took pleasure in the process.

Over the years, to make changes in our home, to create a new ambiance, to be au courant, it was exciting to leaf through magazines, to shop, to talk with friends; and, yes, my sister and later my daughter. It was not a major preoccupation in my life; it didn't call upon my best skills, but feathering the nest did give me a sense of pleasure and satisfaction. It was as if I were doing something that came naturally.

Recently, I've become aware that I no longer derive pleasure from feathering the nest. If I'm attracted to a set of dishes in a display or see a beautiful piece of furniture, the inner pressure to acquire it is no longer there. I no longer ask my daughter what color carpeting to get for my den. I like my furnishings, and there is no excitement attached to making changes, as there was in the past. Is there an internal pressure to feather nests at certain periods of time as there is for birds to feather their nests at a fixed time in their pregnancy?

There is a feeling of loss attached to no longer feeling that inner urge, just as there are many other feelings of loss as we age – the loss of our youthful vitality, our reproductive function, the loss of loved ones. We cope with these losses in various ways.

Are there gains along with the losses? To some degree, yes – in the case of feathering the nest, some relief from the instinctual pressure, from the competitive factor that is part of the nesting process in our culture, and maybe among the birds, too. There is also the freedom to fill the gap, with other interests and pursuits – to say nothing of the money that is saved to use for other urges and purposes – perhaps to help the next generation to feather their nests.

A ROSE IN BLOOM

Rose came into our family life one summer at our beach house. We lived in a large, three-story house on the Atlantic Ocean. There were lots of us – my parents, my sister and brother-in-law and their daughter and my family – my husband and our two children. Although we weren't all there at the same time, we wanted to be there – the house drew all of us like a magnet. From the perspective of time, I can say we lived together in relative, yes relative, harmony.

Although we all did our share of the work involved in running the house, most of us went into the city to work almost every day – so we needed some additional help.

So, along came Rose! A tall, soft-spoken African-American woman from South Carolina. She was 28 years old at the time.

The children hid under the porch the afternoon we met Rose for the first time; they didn't want a stranger to join our family, especially since she was going to "sleep in"- as the phrase went at that time. They managed to avoid her at first but were seduced by her fabulous cooking and her willingness to satisfy any requests they made for their special favorites. They were also enchanted by her voice – she sang as she worked. Her repertoire was very extensive: Fragments of

"In the cool, cool of the evening..." and "Tenderly.... drift through my mind".

One of Rose's unexpected areas of expertise was as a sex educator. Often, I would come home from work, expecting dinner was almost ready and I would find the children sitting with Rose around the kitchen table, evidently entranced with what they were hearing. Rose knew! Never mind that my husband was a gynecologist and I knew a thing or two too, and we considered ourselves approachable parents, Rose was the sex educator par excellence! She had a boyfriend they learned a lot about and even her sister's sex life was material of discussion. I sometimes shudder to think what all this information added to their sex lives! But Rose's talks remained pretty secret.

Rose was a passionate baseball fan, as we all were – Brooklyn Dodger fans. We felt as if we were part of their team because their business manager lived across the street from us. All the famous players of that time came to swim and relax on the beach – Jackie Robinson, who will always be remembered because he broke the racial barrier and because he was the first black player in the major leagues – Roy Campanella, Carl, Erskine, Gil Hodges – Sometimes these legends in their own era even tossed some balls with the children on the block. Rose was right out there on the street with them. Often, she reported she couldn't sleep at night because of her excitement at being so close to her beloved Dodgers.

When Marc (the oldest child) was about 10, he and Rose made a $1 bet, witnessed and filed in the family safe. Marc bet he would be a major league baseball player. Rose bet he would be a doctor. Rose won the bet and collected the bet, figuring in interest and inflation. We had a party and invited Rose to celebrate Marc's graduation from medical school. Rose wanted to cook a celebration dinner for us, but we insisted that she be a guest and we do the cooking.

We didn't see Rose much after that party. There was the occasional visit and telephone call. Then, one day I made a call and I learned her telephone had been disconnected. I felt a sense of loss, almost as if I had heard that she died. Maybe she had.

But when Rose's name is mentioned in our family, there are smiles, sighs, and strong sense of nostalgia for the Rose that bloomed in our lives those many years ago. The bloom on the Rose has never faded.

January 12, 2017

HOME RUN

At the time of this story, my son Marc was ten years old. He and I were Christmas shopping at Macy's and were looking at sports items. Marc was a passionate Dodger fan at that time and fantasized himself as a member of their team. He always wore a baseball glove and punched into it as he walked around. His good mood changed when he had to put his glove down to try on some jackets. Suddenly, the glove was gone. We looked around for an uncomfortable time and with great anguish on his part, we had to leave without the glove.

The memory of that period of time leaps ahead to several weeks later. Now we are shopping for a new glove, a promised Christmas present. Marc is trying on the gloves on a display table covered with gloves. Suddenly, I hear him scream..."It's my glove, I found my glove!". He was convinced it was his glove for sale!

After some time, the manager was convinced it was Marc's glove because he was able to recall every indentation, every spot that was faded, even a small tear near the thumb. I can't tell you that the glove still exists or that it is a display case in Marc's home nor that even the memory is very prominent in the forefront of our brains but it is there, deeply buried and who can explain why a particular trigger ends in a home run – an idea of this piece of work.

A BRUSH WITH HISTORY

Once on a recent visit, my son, who is interested in genealogy, showed me some census records of a house I had lived in as a child. It was many decades ago, but I remember it well. It was located in Manhattan at 297 East 10th Street (near Avenue A) directly opposite Tompkins Square Park. It was one of a row of small houses and according to the census records my father was the owner.

As a physician, he had his office on the ground floor. Our family occupied the two floors above that and my grandparents occupied the top floor. The basement was rented to tenants unrelated to us. I have lived in New York all of my long life and remember all the various homes I've had, but none so vividly as the house on 10th Street.

Although he had heard the story many times, when he showed me his Internet finding, I told Marc again some of my favorite stories of that house, often dramatically recounted by my father. This was a quiet neighborhood at that time, but, at one point, my father began getting complaints from neighbors about noise emanating from our basement. When he went down to investigate he found three printing presses and several printers hard at work on a publication. The head of the project was Leon Trotsky. I don't know how my father dealt with the situation but he always implied that he had a role in giving Trotsky some safe haven in his exile. Later, of course, Trotsky went to Mexico where he was murdered in 1940.

While Marc was still visiting me, his son (my grandson) invited us to dinner on 7th Street and Avenue A, his favorite Greek restaurant.

After dinner, the three generations walked nearby to 10th Street and Avenue A. The house at 297 is still there, unchanged. To my astonishment, there's a doctor's sign exactly where my father's sign used to hang.

There's a real difference that came to my mind. The neighborhood is now a hot real estate location, dubbed ABC. My father probably purchased 297 for thousands; it now is valued in the millions. Unfortunately, only the memory, precious as it is, belongs to me…not the house.

New York, April 2015

NOW AND THEN

On their recent visit to New York, I joined Marc and Becky, my son and daughter-in-law, on a trip to the Museum of Natural History. When my children were growing up we lived only five short blocks from the museum.

As we went in, Marc steered us to the evolution exhibit. My husband would spend a lot of time helping him acquire some understanding of the evolutionary theory of human development. Leon was so passionate about the time they spent at this exhibit that Marc still has a residue of that passion. We speculated about how technology would affect man's continuing development, just as tools and machinery had in the past.

Next, we all chose to visit our friends, the dinosaurs. Just as many children do, Marc had learned all their names and would proudly show off his knowledge, just as I was proud of his knowledge. An interesting lecturer told us about a female dinosaur, about her structure, her habits, etc. He encouraged questions, and my question was about how dinosaurs mated. He shrugged that one off.

Like everyone else, we took pictures, so Becky texted a photo of the three of us in front of one of dinosaurs to her son in Paris. His response was immediate. He said, "But now YOU are the dinosaurs!"

SEX AND SEX THERAPY

Drs. Shirley and Leon Zussman

AS TIME GOES BY (SEX THERAPY)

It's 1957 – I am at a posh restaurant in New York. I delight in having my handsome husband sitting next to me. On his right is the first director of the Human Sexuality Center at LIJ Hillside Center. She is charming all of us. Next to her is the couple that contributed a million dollars to fund the Center. They are our hosts tonight.

Across the table form me are our guests of honor, William Masters and Virginia Johnson. Their work has started the world talking about sex, sex, sex. It is a time at the height of their celebrity. As a newcomer to the field of sex therapy, I can't believe I am having dinner in their company.

My seat at the table faces the wide door that opens into the restaurant. As my glance falls in that direction I see Margaret Mead coming through the door, followed by a group of about six, all of them in colorful ethnic attire. I think there should be a band beating drums. Dr. Mead moves in a slow, measured way towards her table. She is facing in my direction and notices my smile of recognition. She stops and remarks:

"How nice to see you, Shirley, and in such good company". Masters and Johnson rise to greet her, and they address each other as

Maggie, Ginny, and Bill. I whisper to my husband that I can't believe I'm a part of this scene. Is it really happening?

As she moves on, I am asked how I know Margaret Mead. I explain that a few years ago, I was working on my doctoral dissertation. The topic I chose was **Husbands in the Delivery Room**, a popular practice today but considered radical at that time by both prospective parents and obstetricians.

I wanted to explore delivery customs in other cultures; so, feeling very courageous, I arranged a consultation with Margaret Mead, considered a leading authority in the field of anthropology and revered as a faculty member at Columbia University. (Despite her status, she never became a professor because no women were given that rank then!).

Dr. Mead was interested in my work and became a member of my Doctoral Committee. She opened doors for me in many ways. The one I remember most is the door to her office in the Tower of the Museum of Natural History.

As I told my story that evening, I kept pinching myself (and my husband) that I had become a subject of interest to this amazing group.

Now it's 2010 – I am one of the few survivors at the dinner party, perhaps the only one left that remembers that bright, shining moment in time for me. I am having lunch with a young student, who tells me that she wants to become a sex therapist.

At some point I bring up the names Masters and Johnson. She dismisses them as irrelevant today. I don't even try to describe to her their enormous impact on our society. I reflect on how many young people today probably have never even heard their names.

A few days later, a friend brings up the name of Margaret Mead; a name rarely heard today – her books frequently unread. My friend describes Mead's findings as inaccurate. I don't challenge her.

As I sit at my desk, I find myself wondering – What is the fame? What survives? What is knowledge? I have no answers – I decide to go to the gym!

THE SUNDANCE KID

For women of "a certain age" the news that Paul Newman had died meant more than the death of a Hollywood legend, a talented and incredibly handsome actor, a philanthropist, and a daring racer of fast cars.

It meant the loss of the man who was the object of a generation's first sexual stirrings. Who among us didn't have a crush on Paul Newman? Who didn't dream of him at night when the lights were off and the door was closed?

In those adolescent years, a fantasy lover was more satisfying than the pimply boy who made eyes at us in Algebra class or even the boy who didn't know we existed. Even if we were attracted to one boy or another and we were lucky enough that he was attracted to us, there wasn't much we could do about it in those days. Remember?

He couldn't be in our bed, as the case might be today so that was when Paul Newman came into the picture. Not the large-screen moving picture, but that picture in our head, the wonderful imagery called fantasy. It was safe and exciting, and taught us so much about the pleasure our bodies could give us.

As we grew older and found partners in reality, real life and flesh partners, our fantasy life never completely disappeared for we had learned that fantasy could enrich and intensify our sexuality. So, new images emerged from time to time. But for many, Paul Newman never quite disappeared from our fantasy life. Perhaps he never will!

PLAYING DOCTOR

Why do children like to play doctor? I guess a parent could ask, why do children like to play fireman or policeman or ballerina or dentist? And they do! The fact that playing doctor often makes a parent anxious is because, for the parent, it has a sexual implication. Children also play doctor by bandaging fingers and knees and pretending to give medicine and injections; but this is often not the usual association we have to children playing doctor. What parents think about is children examining each other's bodies, pulling down pants or lifting skirts and peeking at genitals. Sometimes it means using a pretend rectal thermometer.

Children often play this form of doctor game because they have a good deal of curiosity about the human body and sexual differences. They are curious about everything in their growing world of experience; but even at a very young age, they sense some mystery about the way they are made. Often they get better answers to their questions about almost everything else than they do about sexual differences. Examining each other is one way of trying to find some answers. Almost everyone remembers playing doctor, even though it occurs so early in life.

Today, sex (and nudity) is everywhere. Even very young children are exposed to sexual matters on TV, in the movies, on the Internet, and as a subject to lively discussion at the dinner table and among nannies on the park bench.

A parent's dilemma is greater than ever as to how to deal with their children's questions. But the real dilemma is their own confusion and their own curiosity. True, today's parents are more knowledgeable and hopefully more comfortable about sexual matters than their own parents were, but a whole new world of sexual experience opens up every day.

How to react to it? How to make sense of it? How to incorporate it into one's own value system? How not to be too turned off by it or too turned on? It may take some time for adults – parents – to integrate this explosion of sexual matters and to help young children cope with what they see and hear from every direction; but in the meantime, my guess is that playing doctor may get a lot more interesting.

FIFTY QUESTIONS

Everyone expresses amazement that *Fifty Shades of Grey* and its sequels have sold many millions of copies all over the world. Yes, sex sells, but these numbers are very rare in any category of the book market.

The story itself is a simple one; and in a way, the characters are simple people – except for the fact that Christian Grey is extremely rich and handsome beyond description, but isn't that a common fantasy of the single girl? Anastasia, a 21-year-old college student is not pursuing Christian. She meets him by chance when she helps out a friend who is ill. The friend needs to interview Christian for a student newspaper and Anastasia volunteers to take on the assignment. Christian seems benign; she is a literary major who likes to curl up at night with a British classic. Anastasia is a virgin and has never even held hands with a man.

In the beginning, they are like two exaggerated characters you might find in a summer beach novel. The first hint of something dark comes when Christian sends her a first edition of Thomas Hardy's Tess of the D'Urbervilles, the subject of Anastasia's senior thesis. He has brought attention to the question from the text, "Why didn't you tell me there was danger?"

The danger from Christian is his compulsive desire to have sadomasochistic sexual experiences, with the female partner completely submissive. His traumatic childhood is given as an explanation of this compulsive desire.

There is no evidence of force or brutality or disregard of her unwillingness to participate in this behavior. He makes it clear what the terms are and requests her to sign a contractual agreement to participate.

Why does Anastasia agree? Why do millions of readers, probably many of them women, identify with her, get pleasure from the detailed account of the pain and lack of control? Her willingness to submit?

There are no doubts many theories and conjectures about the popularity of this book. What makes it so compelling? In this age of the active, assertive female, fighting to break the glass ceiling and gain control, what attracts her to Anastasia's submission?

What came to mind is the research of my colleague, Dr. Barbara Hariton. Thirty or more years ago, she wrote a doctoral dissertation about women's sexual fantasies. She studied a group of suburban, middle-class women who described themselves as happily married and enjoying their sexual life with their husbands.

Dr. Hariton's focus was on the sexual fantasies of these women. She reported that a majority of them described that, during sex with their husbands, they frequently fantasized about being sexually overpowered by a strong, powerful male, or group of men, who were neither brutal nor frightening in any way. These encounters were not viewed by any of the women as safe.

There are reports of subsequent research that has confirmed Dr. Hariton's findings of women's sexual fantasies – even in a time of even further liberation of women.

What does it mean? Is the research too limited? Does it serve some biological purpose for the male to be sexually powerful to guarantee the continuation of the species?

The questions interest me more than the book.

WHAT MAKES FOR HOT SEX?

Surprisingly, it is not always with Mr. Right. As a matter of fact, an inappropriate partner or an unavailable one often fuels the fire of sexual desire more than someone who meets the requirements of the ideal partner.

Would the story of Romeo and Juliet enthrall us to the same degree if theirs were not a clandestine affair? Would the outcome of that tragic tale be the same if their parents were not engaged in a vendetta that made their love prohibitive?

Then there's the story of "Looking for Mr. Goodbar". Remember? Diane Keaton plays the role of a conventional, compassionate teacher deciding to be her "own girl". In the murky nightclubs she explores, she finds excitement with dangerous and unpredictable men and spurns the Mr. Right in her life. This story, too, ends in disaster.

But many of us experience yearning for an unavailable partner, pine over an ambivalent lover, or engage in risk-taking sexual encounters at some time in their lives. How can we explain the excitement in such behavior? And the intensity of the sexual feelings connected with the experience?

It's not unlike other ways in which some people, especially in their younger years, break the rules by driving too fast, drinking too much, or getting involved in drugs.

Taking risks seems to offer a feeling of power, a sense of entitlement to engage in behavior that has been prohibited in the past.

If the risks involved in the area of sexual behavior haven't led to disastrous or very painful consequences, most people move on to want sexual experiences to be part of an intimate, secure relationship.

Memories of these experiences often linger on and may trigger excitement in fantasy life and even add excitement to sex with Mr. Right!

WORK ADDICTION – NO TIME FOR LOVE

Are you a workaholic? For the past years, wives complained that their husbands were addicted to work. Some wives even threatened to end the marriage because addiction to work and long hours at the office left no room for companionship and the pursuit of shared pleasures. As of sex – "too tired" – "tomorrow" – were the common excuses. And there was always, almost always, office work to be completed at home.

But not only wives complained, husbands accused their wives of putting the care of children and household chores ahead of them to such a degree that the relationship became sterile, devoid of time together to play, to talk, to hold each other, to make love.

With an increasing number of women working outside of the home, and still having tasks at home, we are hearing more about work addiction on the part of women, with more frequent feelings on the part of men of being rejected and neglected. Men are becoming more involved in helping with house work at home, while the women of the family sit at their computer – late into the night.

Of course, high-pressure careers often demand long hours, travel, and intense involvement. The troubled economy may demand

44

more involvement to avoid losing one's job.

However, sometimes the investment of excess time and energy is to meet the workaholic's needs, rather than the job's requirements. People addicted to work see themselves as having little option, stating they have to get the job done, or they feel restless or on edge if they are not busy.

What are some motivations that drive some men and women "beyond the call of duty"? Of course, the lure of money – "making it big" is a common motivation – but even millionaires are often work addicts. There are other motives, of course – the attempt to deal with low self-esteem, which is bolstered by always being busy. Another not uncommon reason for being addicted to work in the fear of intimacy – of getting close to someone else.

There is no AA for work addiction. Our culture worships success, money, and power. We admire people who work hard and have contempt (usually hidden) for those who are idle or unemployed. But, as the technological revolution makes us feel more isolated, there is a new surge of interest in seeking connection, spirituality, and meaning in our lives. Couples need to talk (an important aspect of intimacy) to find their individual path to feeling less alone.

IS YOUR BEDROOM ANOTHER WORKPLACE?

"The bedroom isn't just for sleeping anymore". That's part of a popular commercial that shows furniture that can convert the bedroom to an office, a computer center, or an entertainment area (Stereo, TV, VCR, DVD, etc.) In lieu of making love, many modern couples use the bedroom to make more money, by extending their working hours. Papers, disks, files fill the bedroom space while one or both partners spend long hours in front of their computer.

Instead of entertaining each other by holding, stroking, lying quietly together or sharing intimate thoughts and feelings one or both are immersed in a soap opera of the latest sexual exploits of the rich and famous.

Often a beloved pet, either canine or feline, shares the bedroom or even the bed and may be getting most of the petting and hugging. Sex therapists sometimes discover that a pet sleeps between a couple, and serving as a barrier between them as an unspoken way of avoiding each other. Small children sometimes serve the same purpose.

What about your bedroom – does it have a computer, a TV set, a motley assortment of papers and books? Have you settled the issue of king size, queen size, double or separate bed?

Is sex another work activity that takes place in the bedroom?

Separate bedrooms are a luxury of modern life. In the 15th and 16th centuries, people lived in general purpose rooms as they still do in some societies (and in studio apartment?) They ate, slept, entertained and worked in the same room. Beds were often collapsible and were set up as needed. Many centuries were required to develop the concept of the bedroom as a private sanctuary. Enjoy it as such – don't make your bedroom the public, general-purpose room of the 15th Century.

STARTING OVER

Today, there are widowed, divorced, or separated people who yearn to find an intimate partner again. Or perhaps there is a partner, but a physical intimacy no longer exists.

Because our society constantly emphasizes that sex and love are only for the young and beautiful, many older people withdraw from seeking a new partner or engaging in any form of sexual activity with the partner sharing their bed. They are afraid to risk rejection, experience performance anxiety and are reluctant to expose themselves as less attractive and desirable than they were in their younger years.

If they do meet someone or if they yearn to resume an intimate relationship with a long-term partner, the fear of how they will perform haunts them. Sex in the media today is portrayed as a "how to" activity that only involves younger men and women.

The famous sex researchers, Masters and Johnson, described that long periods of sexual abstinence can develop into a form of atrophy not unlike what an athlete experiences when he gives up his sport over a long period of time. He needs to go slowly to regain his former confidence. A certain amount of awkwardness is to be expected just like it might be on a new job, meeting new people, or learning all over again a long-forgotten skill. Alcohol doesn't help. Shakespeare knew that "It provokes the desire – but dulls the performance".

"Women often worry that intercourse may be uncomfortable because vaginal tissues can by dry and brittle from disuse. It is a good idea to visit a gynecologist. If this could be a problem, it can be easily corrected. Don't wait until an encounter occurs; be prepared!" Masturbation helps to keep the tissues moist, too.

Focusing on the pleasure, not the goal is a good way to start over. Enjoy touching, kissing, and tasting the warmth of a partner's body next to yours. Explore!

What's the hurry? It is not as if you're a teenager and your parents will be home from the movies any minute. And your kids have left home long ago.

IS THERE A MALE MENOPAUSE?

There was a time not so long ago when women never talked about menopause and never used the word, even with close friends or even an intimate partner. They regarded it as a condition that was inevitable and generally considered that, once they reached menopause around the age of fifty, they were "over the hill" – especially in the area of their sexuality. With the flowering of the feminist movement, menopause came out of the closet.

Books about menopause became best sellers and it was a popular topic on radio and TV talk shows. Even the pharmaceutical industry became involved offering new formulas to ease severe symptoms from which some women suffered. Gradually, women began to believe that there was life possible after menopause – even an active sex life. Recently, some of the attention focused on female menopause has shifted to men. The question has been asked, "Is there a male menopause?"

In the true sense of the word, the word menopause means the end of menses and men do not menstruate. On a hormonal level, females experience an abrupt ending of estrogen, which causes many of the symptoms that women sometimes experience. Men don't have this abrupt ending to the production of testosterone, the hormone responsible in the male and female sex drive. There may be a gradual decline over the years, but this decline doesn't occur in all men. But like women, men do age as time goes by. At about the same age as women experience menopause, they start to lose some of their strength and vigor, lose some of their hair and they, too, develop wrinkles. Of course, exercise and healthy diet may do a lot in both sexes to postpone signs of aging – their sex drive may diminish, but there is no scientific evidence that is tied to a decrease in their hormonal decline. But many men do report what we might label a mid-life crisis around the same time as women experience menopause. There may be many psychological reasons for this state – often tied to awareness that life is passing them by, they haven't realized their dreams, the nest is empty, and life has lost some of its possibilities, its promise.

Women, too, experience some of these feelings; but in recent years, many women feel a new sense of freedom and opportunity – that Margaret Mead described as menopausal zest. It seems to me that we are now into a New Age, that the mid-life crisis may still occur, but perhaps not in the fifties – but with our increasing longevity, many years later. I often remember that a century ago women died in their late forties – they probably never experienced menopause and men's lives were much shorter then too. With the possibility of an extended lifespan, we need to not only focus on enriching our personal lives but making the world a better place in which everyone can live a fulfilling life.

TOUCHING

We never outgrow our need for touching. The very first experience we have with another human being is being touched. We learn about love and pleasure by being stroked, caressed, held, and rocked. Baby animals die if the mother does not lick and stroke them. Even human babies sometimes do not survive if they are deprived of tender loving care. Toddlers, taking their first steps quickly, run back to their mother's sheltering arms to be picked up and caressed. The imprint of these first experiences with physical intimacy or the lack of it never leaves us.

You lovers spend countless hours touching and holding each other. All the love songs of every generation say hold me, take me in your arms, and let me hold your hand.

Most other relationships require that we keep our distance – hands off – don't touch, for most of us the only opportunity we have to touch and be touched is with our lover – our husband or wife. Children and old people need touching too. Yet how much we sometimes neglect touching or being touched.

Often touching is restricted to a few moments of lovemaking in bed instead of being an important part of our lives. In the course of my work, I often hear patients' express how much they want and need to be caressed, stroked, and held. Men often fear to express their need for touching because they fear it will be interpreted as passivity. Both men and women, young and old, should keep in touch... You never outgrow your need for touching!

HEAVY PETTING

Tim had visited quite a few times, and we had established some kind of relationship. He had even taken me for a walk once or twice when my lady was tired or maybe just glad of a break from our usual routine. It was a treat for me, because he walked on different streets and didn't stop to look at shop windows.

But this was different. Tim had moved in! It wasn't just his physical presence around so much of the time. It was his clothes in her closet, his shoes and socks under her bed, and the new smells that permeated our place.

But it was the situation in the bedroom that disturbed me the most. I had always slept at the foot of my lady's bed. Sometimes she'd pull me under the covers with her, hug me and shower me with kisses, and even let me stay next to her all night.

I had even discovered that certain situations led to her wanting me close. Sometimes it was because she was sad. I could feel her hot tears wetting my fur, sometimes she was happy and she'd hold me in the air and we would dance to her happy laughter. Sometimes she would ignore me, and I knew then that it was my job to comfort her. I learned how to be pretty good at that. But since Tim moved in, things were different. True, he had slept over a few times before. I had been polite enough to our guest to let him have complete privacy. But that didn't mean I was going to give up my proprietary rights.

Why they were getting undressed, I jumped on the bed and waited till they got in. My lady would pet me and kiss me good night and a few times she and Tim played with me under the covers.

But I couldn't deal with it when I saw how close they got in bed. Often, they looked as if there were struggling, and I would growl and bark and jump on Tim to protect my lady. At first Tim would laugh; but when I perfected my strategy to separate them, Tim started to pick me up and put me on the floor. Once or twice, he carried me out of the room. My lady would protest and tell Tim, "He'll get used to not being #1". But, will I?

THE BUTTOCKS – HIGH STYLE!

Men seem to be fascinated with all parts of a women's body, but derrieres and breasts evidently get particular attention – not only from the male sex but from the fashion industry as well. Having practically bared breasts in recent times, attention has now shifted to buttocks. What's so intriguing about that part of a woman's body?

Well, first of all, like breasts, they come in varying sizes and shapes. They seem to vary somewhat from one ethnic group to another, providing variety to the observer. They also sway, move, and swing – providing variety that way as well.

The tight jeans of today's styles help to draw attention to that part of the body, but there is nothing new about that. Previous generations of women emphasized buttocks with heavy padding – and what about the bustle? But we've added the thong, and we all know that the thong is part of our history.

Interest in the buttocks often starts in childhood. It's a part of the body that can't be seen – it is a source of curiosity and sensual pleasure. Toilet training focuses a lot of attention on our rear ends. Children are told it is naughty and not be tolerated if that part of the body is exposed, but it doesn't prevent them from trying and seeing the reaction.

Women notice men's buttocks too and men's fashions caters to that interest as well with tight jeans and low waistlines even exposing underwear and the "crack". Which all points to be an increasing recognition of the fascination of the human body! What's next? What will happen to fashion if nudity becomes the new thing?

OVER THE HILL

There are many myths and misconceptions in the area of sexuality, but one of the most persistent is that menopause marks the end of a woman's sexual interest and desirability. Since the average age of menopause is fifty-one, it is around that age that she sees herself and fears that she is seen as "over the hill", sexually speaking. This misconception has been reinforced by our current society's message that sex is only for the young and beautiful, and young is being defined as younger and younger, and beautiful is being defined as more and more beautiful (and thinner and thinner).

There is a frantic pursuit on the part of many women and men, too, for maintaining and recapturing youth and beauty. Anti-wrinkle creams, and who hasn't used them, fill shelves even in supermarkets. The newest is the promise of a stem cell product that will keep skin eternally young. There is a staggering increase in the demand for plastic surgery for every part of the body (the most recent in popularity is the reconstruction of the belly button). It is not only women who beat a path to the surgeon's operating table, but men too want to restore their youthful look and even improve on the original model.

A popular procedure is "enhancing" and lengthening their penis, thus reinforcing another myth that "bigger is better". Although some motive for pushing back the clock to achieve a more youthful look may be that youth and beauty are valued in the workplace as well, much of the motivation seems to be to preserve and enhance a sexual image. Yet, there is no solid evidence that sexual interest and activity ceases and declines markedly as women and men reach fifty and beyond. As a matter of fact, evidence points to the contrary.

In the 1950s, Alfred Kinsey, in his groundbreaking book, The Sexual Behavior of the Human Female, was the first to publish a survey of sexuality in older women. The findings revealed that women retain sexual capacity and sexual interest. The most recent study reported in The New York Times a short time ago found that most Americans remain sexually active into their early sixties, and nearly half continue to have sex into their early seventies. Of course, sexual interest and activity during the menopausal period and beyond is extremely variable, depending on many psychological and physiological factors, even on whether there is an available partner. There was a time at the beginning of the Twentieth Century when women died at an average age of forty-eight and did not even live long enough to experience menopause. It is not long since menopause was a word never mentioned until the feminist movement brought it out of the closet. With the Boomers now reaching fifty in large numbers, maybe they won't need to feel over the hill, but rather will climb mountains to a new definition of sex and beauty.

GLAMOUR

THE BEST SEX ADVICE FROM THE LAST CENTURY –

GLAMOUR MAGAZINE, DECEMBER 2009

Former GLAMOUR sex columnist Shirley Zussman, 95(!), shares what's better and worse for women now, and how to have a blissed-out sex life.

Mikki Halpin

BIGGEST ADVANCE

Women are More Body Confident

"How to have an orgasm was the top question during my Glamour days", says Zussman, who's still a practicing sex therapist. "But today women know how to make themselves feel good..." There's only one problem: "Somehow they still aren't always comfortable conveying that to their partner". Zussman suggests using action instead of words. "Words can sound like criticism", she admits "Instead, put his hand on yours while you do what you like – he'll pick things up."

BIGGEST SETBACK

All Those Gadgets!

"The most frequent problem I see in my practice today is lack of desire", says Zussman. "A lot of that has to do with the never-ending workday we have with phones and computers. They are very seductive". Bedrooms used to be just for sleeping and sex, and that's how it should be, she says. "Don't let your bedroom become an office."

WHAT'S THE SAME

The Importance of Your Sexual Health

"We learned early on that many sex problems aren't just in your head; there is a real underlying cause, such as side effects from medication decreasing your libido", says Zussman. "That's still true". So it's important to make regular visits to your GP and ob-gyn. "Being diligent now is key to having a healthy body – and great sex – for the future", she says.

Here's What a 100-Year-Old Sex Therapist Thinks is Wrong With Sex Today

Time Magazine (time.com) *Charlotte Alter, Diane Tsai*

Aug 20, 2014

She was born before the invention of the stop sign, but sex therapist Shirley Zussman has some thoughts on 'hooking up.' "I don't think it's as frantic as casual sex was in the sixties," she says, noting that modern 'hooking up' isn't as exciting without the context of a sexual revolution. Besides, she adds: "In the long run, sexual pleasure is just one part of what men and women want from each other."

At 100, Dr. Zussman is still a practicing sex therapist in New York City. In the 50-plus years since she began counseling people about all things related to sex, Dr. Zussman has witnessed everything from the legalization of the contraceptive birth control pill in 1960 (she started in sex therapy shortly afterwards) to the AIDS epidemic in the 1980s to the rise of internet porn in the new millennium.

She's one of the oldest sex therapists in the world, but that might be the least extraordinary thing about her life and career. Born at the beginning of World War I, she graduated from Smith College in 1934, in the same class as Julia Child. Zussman was mentored through her graduate dissertation by Margaret Mead, and in the 1960s learned about sex therapy from Masters and Johnson, the inspiration for the Showtime series *Masters of Sex*. Her husband, a gynecologist, performed one of the first legal abortions in New York.

Here's what she has to say about casual sex, cell phones, and how our hectic work lives are changing our attitudes toward sex.

On how being busy hurts your sex life:

"The use of time is very different in our society today. People are busy all the time. That was not true when I was growing up. At this stage of our development, we want to cover everything, we want to know everything, we want to do everything, and there's also [our personal] economy which requires an immense amount of time and effort...There is a limit to how much energy and desire and time you can give to one person when there is all this pressure make more money, to be the CEO, to buy a summer house, people want more and more and more. Desire requires a certain amount of energy.

It's a consequence of being exhausted...The most common problem I see is a lack of desire, a lack of interest. I had a patient say to me, ' I love my husband, I love making love to him, but I come home from work, I've been with people all day, I just want to crash.'"

On an increased openness about sex:

"I don't think that the stigma around sex therapy exists like it was in the early years. People were ashamed they had to go to a psychiatrist or a social worker, because it means they needed help. Many people resist the idea that somebody needs to tell them how to have sex."

"There were changes in the culture, too, there was the sexual revolution. There was the development of the pill, women were freer to not worry so much about getting pregnant, there was every magazine and TV program talking about sex, there was every advertisement using sex to sell their product. There was an overwhelming immersion in the whole idea of getting more pleasure out of sex. It was not just about having babies."

On what she learned from Masters and Johnson:

"They were recognizing that it was not all just glamorous and wonderful to be sexual, but that one almost had to learn to be a good partner...Their way of communicating was one of their greatest contributions, and that was not to talk so much about it, but to start with touching and caressing and stroking and kissing, and not rush for that golden bell in the middle of the carousel. It doesn't start with the man having an erection and then you have intercourse, 1,2,3."

And what she thinks of the TV show:

"I went to the preview party and met some of the actors in it. I was introduced to Michael Sheen, and he knew that I had known Masters and Johnson, so he said 'tell me, how do you think I'm representing him?'

I said, 'I think you're doing a pretty good job, but there's a major difference.' He said, 'what's that?' I said, 'you're handsome.'"

On her weirdest experience in 50 years of sex therapy:

"Someone called me and said he needed some help. He said 'I'm a bad boy and I'm looking for someone for spankings.' I had to make it clear that that's not within my range of expertise."

On the difference between casual sex in the 60s and 'hooking up' today:

"I think there's a big change in the way we view casual sex. In the 60s it wasn't just casual—it was frantic. It was something you expected to happen to you, you wanted it to happen, it was sort of a mad pursuit of sexual pleasure. But I think over time the disadvantages of that kind of behavior began to become apparent. There was the emotional crash-- the intimacy was not there in the way that people need and want. There was a concern about sexual diseases, and then eventually AIDS made a major impact on calming that excitement."

I think what was expected of casual sex – frantic sex-- was something that didn't deliver. Because in the long run, sexual pleasure is just one part of what men and women want from each other. They want intimacy, they want closeness, they want understanding, they want fun, and they want someone who really cares about them beyond just going to bed with them."

I think hooking up includes some aspect of the kind of sex we were just talking about, but in a very much modified, and limited way. It's not as frantic."

On the popularity of oral sex:

"Oral sex was always part of the picture. I think primitive people learned how to get pleasure from oral sex, we just didn't know about it. Oral sex was never talked about in your mother's generation or my mother's generation or my generation in the early days."

On internet pornography:

"There's nothing new about pornography. It's been around since prehistoric days...I think that's a healthy thing that people have the ability and the freedom to allow themselves to fantasize. But I have a number of patients who sit in front of the computer and watch pornography online, and somehow lose interest in seeking a partner. I see that a lot in some single men who don't make the effort to go out in the world to face the issues, face the possible rejection—they satisfy their sexual needs sitting in front of the computer and masturbating."

On living to be 100:

"We've been brainwashed to think that we all become couch potatoes when we're old. You have to have expectations of yourself! You can make friends in many different ways, but you have to make the effort. You can't say 'oh, all my friends died,' or 'they're sick,' or 'they don't want to do what I want to do.' You have to make an effort to find those new people. They don't just come running to your door the way they might have when you were growing up."

On the evils of cell phones:

"I'm shocked at the lack of connection between people because of iPhones. There is so much less of actual physical connection. There's less touching, there's less talking, there's less holding, there's less looking. People get pleasure from looking at each other. From a smile, and touching. We need touching to make us feel wanted and loved. That's lacking so much in this generation. Lack of looking, lack of touching, lack of smiling. I don't get it. I don't get how people aren't missing that, and don't seem to think they are."

TRAVEL ON A TIME MACHINE

"Then There Were Four" and "Very Much in the Moment"

Shirley outside her dormitory

Smith College 1934, 75th class reunion

Tuesday, August 5, 2008

MIRROR, MIRROR ON THE WALL

So, I'm 95. It doesn't seem very different than 85 or 75 – only when I look in the mirror and even the image is so familiar. I've gotten used to the gradual changes over the years. It's the same face, the same familiar expression. What does that expression convey? Why hasn't it changed over the years? It seems to reassure me – tell me that I'm OK that I'm still a lucky lady – so get on with whatever you have in mind.

Would I want to have that image reflect a different Shirley? Of course, over the years, especially in my younger years, I hoped I would see a beautiful face, a face gazed upon with envy by every onlooker.

Would I want that person I see in the mirror to have a different history, different memories? I don't think so. I was born into a loving family, educated, easygoing, loving their lives and without any major problems or traumas.

Would I want to have chosen a different career? Definitely not! I chose the right one for a lifetime, with a moderate amount of success, and even had my fifteen minutes of fame! But, come now, who are you kidding? Of course, you'd want your script to have had some different lines. Of course! I wish I had learned to play a musical instrument, been a talented tennis player, danced more under the stars, sung more songs, had more lovers, kept my husband alive to be by my side in my old age, had him next to me as we flew around the world one more time!

I wish I had had more impact on making the world a better place for my children and grandchildren as they grow old.

But as I look at the mirror one moment longer before I start on my 95th year, I sing to myself, to paraphrase Cole Porter's song, "Luck, be a lady today!"

August 08, 2008

TRAVEL ON A TIME MACHINE

I was ambling down an aisle displaying toys in a neighborhood store, looking for a present for a four-year-old friend. Suddenly, my eyes landed on a package of jacks, in a ziplock bag. They were made of hard plastic and were of different colors. The package also contained a small ball.

As if I were travelling on a time machine, I was on the floor of a cabin in the Adirondack Mountains. It was one of the cabins of Camp Red Wing, a girls' camp on Schroon Lake, I was one of six eight-year-old girls playing jacks. I could feel the rough texture of the floorboards on my bare legs, spread out so that the jacks were close to my body. These jacks were metal and not colored.

I could see the white shine of the shirts worn by the cabin-mates, as they sat in a circle around me, transfixed by my hand holding the ball some of their names flashed through my mind, the way a long forgotten melody sometimes appears. I could even see beyond the circle of girls, the narrow cots, the unadorned windows, framing the beautiful foliage of a summer day in the woods.

That eight-year-old girl didn't know or even think then about the woman she was to become or the life she would lead. But the woman she became carries her around in some special part of her memory, and it only takes a package of jacks or some other trigger to bring her back to life for a bright, shining moment.

ANOTHER RIDE ON A TIME MACHINE

His name leaped out at me from the obituary column of my morning newspaper. An electric shock vibrated through my body as I read that he was 96 years old at the time of his death. He had been married for 60 years, had children, grandchildren, and great-grandchildren and had been a successful businessman.

As if I were on a time machine, he and I were on a beautiful lake in the Adirondack Mountains. He was 18 years old and I was 16. We had just finished a long swim and we were slightly out of breath, watching the sunset. I could feel the wetness of my bathing suit, the sand on my feet and on my shoulders.

The majestic mountains surrounding the lake were like walls providing a private space in which the two of us seemed to exist. Private moments were in marked contrast to the busy, noisy action-filled days of our roles as counselors at a summer camp. So we rested quietly, only the signing of birds, breaking the silence.

He turned towards me, as if he wanted to say something. Perhaps it was accidental, because we had never touched each other before, but within a moment we were holding each other, caressing each other. I could feel the droplets of water on our bodies mingling together. A wonderful feeling erupted within me.

A short time later, the summer was over, and I was about to begin my freshman year at college in Massachusetts. I never saw him again. For many months, he inhabited my fantasy life. I dreamed that we would be together, sharing the pleasures of new experiences.

And now I read that he was dead. I was 94 years old as I read that notice. But as I traveled on a time machine that morning, we were swimming in the cool waters of a beautiful lake – he was 18, I was 16 – both of us joyfully unaware of life's inevitable stages.

LOST IN TRANSITION

There are many losses on the bumpy road to old age. Everyone struggles to avoid, or more realistically, to postpone the loss of youthful beauty and vigor, of fading vision and hearing, and the dreaded loss of memory. Then, there is the tragic loss of cherished family and friends.

In recent years, there have been some contributions that have helped to make some of the bumps less traumatic – medical advances, more knowledge about the role of nutrition and exercise, cosmetic surgery. But this is a piece about loss, not new horizons, for the elderly.

For me, a major loss is the gradual erosion of ambition – that passion to achieve a particular goal and the willingness to work hard to achieve it. It seems to me I've always set goals for myself and enjoyed the process of getting thee. Like most things in life, getting there is half the fun. That is what I miss. I have to acknowledge that on some level. I feel as ambitious as ever, but the reality is that old age puts a roadblock on getting there.

Many people welcome an end to the "fire in the belly" – that pressure to perform and achieve. They are the ones who look forward to retirement and its freedom from stress. Sometimes, they find even freedom has its own stress and the process of getting old doesn't stop.

Then there are those, like me, who need to find avenues where that fire brightens their older years, even though its light is not as bright, its heat is not as warming; but as Edna St. Vincent Millay once put it in a different context, "But ah my foes, and oh, my friends, it gives a lovely light".

SO YOU THINK YOU CAN DANCE?

Yes, you can!

On a recent trip to Florida, I visited a posh country club, all of whose members appeared to be senior citizens. Many of them have partners, short or long term.

An interesting contrast to the sea of gray hair and stooped shoulders was the club's staff, young and vibrant men and women from around the world. They seemed to have formed a friendly, caring bond with the people they serve.

Many of the club members are retired people, seeking not only relief from winter's chill but a milieu to make new friends and enjoy activities, both old and new to them.

The dining room had a festive air and an extravagant display of fine food and wine. Of course, there was no way to know how many of these guests need special diets, preventing them from partaking of the tempting food offered. As they came into the dining room or left it later on, they stopped to greet friends at the tables scattered around the room like hosts at a private party.

Adjacent to the dining room was a lounge. Not everyone settled there after dinner, but I soon identified those who did, as having dancing feet. Couple after couple walked over to one end of the room, where there was a platform. There was music, a three-piece ensemble, a talented, exuberant singer, all of whom seemed to be enjoying themselves as much as the dancers. For me, it was like watching high-quality entertainment. Indeed, these people could dance! They moved to the beat of the music with an expertise that made me speculate that they had taken expensive lessons to become so expert, just as they took lessons to improve their golf game or their bridge skills.

I felt pleasure watching my 90-year-old brother twirling his spirited partner around the dance floor, executing intricate steps with ease and grace. I felt a pang of envy that I did not have a partner to swing to the beat. It was not a wish that I were young again; but a wish that at 94, I could be sharing the pleasure of this experience, rather than being a spectator.

Of course, these privileged people are not free of the fears and anxieties we all have. They, too, mourn the loss of their youth and vigor, the death of loved ones, the aches and pains of aging, the woes of the world – but for some shining moments in time, it's "Let's Face the Music and Dance!"

SOUP'S ON!

I was an intern at the family agency and could hardly believe my good fortune. Now I was dealing with real people rather than studying case histories in the classroom. Thus began my professional career and much of what I learned in that far away time has remained with me.

What has also been a dividend from that time is a friendship that developed with another intern in that office. In the many years since that time, during the incredible changes in our lives and in the wide, wide world, our love for each other had not diminished. Together, we gained some confidence in our professional selves. We also reveled in being young and carefree.

Although in later years we traveled to faraway and exotic places – at that time our travel was to singles resorts in the Catskills and Adirondacks, citadels of dreams that no longer exist in the era of modern transportation.

We grew older. We got jobs. We got married. We moved out of the sheltering arms of our parents' homes. We learned how to cook and combined being wives and dedicated workers. Our husbands became part of our close friendship and we added children to our circle.

Our friends moved to Westchester; we stayed in Manhattan. We exchanged visits as often as we could. I remember some feeling of difference in their lifestyle. Their friends seemed more suburban, more interested in their homes, their gardens, their carpools. They didn't travel into Manhattan as much for theatre, museums, and concerts.

But, despite what felt somewhat like their complacency, we remained closely bound by our political passion. We lived in turbulent times – the Great Depression, World War II, the labor movement's thrust towards unions, the left wings – "We Shall Overcome". We joined in the struggles. We wanted to change the world as our children would do a generation later. We marched in parades and sang songs of protest that still ring in my ears.

We got even older. My husband died. I went to her husband's 100th birthday party. A few days ago, my friend called me to say that her husband died at the age of 104. Until the end, he had been playing bridge, taking art classes, and enjoying life with his partner for 73 years.

With all the memories stirred up, all the feeling the news of a long-time friend evoked, why did I smell the rich aroma of my friend's mother's cabbage soup? As interns we would drop into her mother's apartment for dinner, which was near our office. Clearer than any other memory, I was sitting at her dining room table, sipping the soup, keenly aware at some level that all of life, with its infinite possibilities, stretched ahead of me.

CANE AND ABLE

There was a time in my life, long, long ago when the word cane conjured up an image of a sugary, red and white striped stick with a curve at its end. These candy canes were a special treat during Christmas and usually disappeared after the holiday season was over.

Years later, when I was still very young, I was occasionally aware that a raggedly old man or woman was limping down the street, leaning heavily on what was referred to as a cane. It was usually not on my street that I saw this sight. It had nothing to do with me.

If I had grown up in any other period of history, canes would have been a very common sight. Throughout every period of history, canes were everywhere. Even primitive man probably used a stick or branch to clear his way or protect him from danger.

Canes and walking sticks, as they were often referred to served many functions from weapon, status, and as a fashion accessory. They were originally made from bamboo or other plants but evolved into elaborate and decorative objects – but somehow the name cane survived.

By the end of World War II, when there was a major cultural change in our society, canes seem to have disappeared. It was the Jazz

Age, the age of the flappers, an age of new freedom in dress and morals.

Recently, canes have come out of the closet. They are as ubiquitous – yes, on my street and in my neighborhood – just like cell phones, dogs on leashes, and baby strollers. Sometimes, one of these is seen in combination with a cane.

The people using canes today are not as old and ragged as they had been in my youth. If they're old, I thought, old has a different look. As I see them in my neighborhood, they certainly aren't ragged. And now there are younger people among the cane users.

The thought enters my mind now and then that given the proliferation of cane users, selling canes might be a profitable investment. I was not conscious that using a cane might be a good personal investment, even though I jokingly referred to the fact that I walked like a drunken sailor.

One day, in a visit to my internist, I mentioned my shaky balance. He immediately recommended a cane, gravely telling me he didn't want to meet me in the emergency room after a fall.

It took me about two years to act on my doctor's order. After I bought a cane, it took me months before I actually carried it out of my building onto my street. Yes, it makes me feel more secure as I rush around from one activity to another. Yes, I'm getting used to using my cane – but I'm still trying to get used to the change in my self-image brought about by the cane.

OPEN SESAME

I turn the key and the door opens. I walk into my office waiting room. Although I have not redecorated it for a few years, I think of it as more attractive than any of the waiting rooms where I have waited as a patient.

I feel proud as I look around. I am a Master of the Universe here. Not a Wall Street Master of the Universe, but a respected and successful member of my profession. Here I have the pleasure of doing work that contributes a rich dimension to my life. Here I have earned money that has contributed to my sense of self-worth.

I am of a generation in which middle class women generally did not work after college. Their chief goal was to marry and have children. I wanted that too, but I always wanted to pursue a career.

Here in this office, my husband and I had adjoining suites; and for a time, collaborated as a sex therapy team. He would be proud of me that I continue in this space and purchased the office when the building became a co-op. I rent the extra suite and so have some sense of being a businessperson.

The one disturbing feeling that comes over me from time to time is that my life here will come to an end – which I will become too feeble in mind and body to be a Master of the Universe and patients will no longer come through that door.

But until that day comes and I put my keys in the lock, I will be a Master of My Universe and I feel fulfilled.

ONCE UPON A MATTRESS

A few weeks ago, I purchased a new mattress for my bed. I had recently bought one for the bed in my guest room and I decided I deserved equal treatment.

Mattresses come in all sizes, variations in quality, differences in firmness, and a nice variation in price. The salesman who was helping me make a decision emphasized the importance of durability in choosing a mattress. He was proud that his store's policy was to guarantee that the mattress would be in good condition after five years or your money would be refunded, or you would get a replacement.

At 95 years of age, I would have preferred a guarantee of my survival to use the mattress – I didn't even consider the idea of it being replaced.

My age however didn't seem to get in the way of my selecting a high quality mattress, at an exorbitant price. Evidently, I still cling to the belief that the best is the cheapest in the long run. I think, too, that age has heightened my sense of entitlement – that I deserve the best.

Although I looked forward to the delivery of the mattress, so that I could enjoy its comfort, I feared that my sleep would be disturbed by concern about the hole in my budget that this purchase had made. But, no, I had no such concern.

As I drifted off to sleep, my thoughts focused on the virginal twin sized bed I had slept in growing up in my parents' home.

I smiled as I recalled the squeaky iron bed I had recently slept in at my college reunion. Had I really slept on a bed like that for four years in my turbulent youth?

The king sized bed I had shared with my husband loomed in my dreamlike state. It took up most of the space, deservedly, so we both thought, in the bedroom of our first apartment. After his death, I bought a queen sized bed. The king had died, but not my expectation that there would be someone else to share my bed.

When I made this recent purchase I chose a full size mattress – no return to the virginal twin size bed of my youth, but evidently the expectation of sharing my bed was no longer there.

Interestingly, after a few weeks I am glad I bought a new mattress – the cost is forgotten, I'm enjoying its comfort, but I feel a sense of regret that I did not buy a queen sized one. Even without a partner I evidently still want to feel like a queen!

AS TIME GOES BY

Shirley Zussman

You have to a cock-eyed optimist not to believe that at an advanced age your time on this earth is pretty limited. You can wonder why you've been allotted so many years, but after a while you take it pretty much for granted that lady luck is on your side and maybe you still have some days, months, even years.

So, how to use whatever time may lie ahead? Grandiose ideas emerge that involved places that you have never seen, (but always wanted to), projects you still want to develop, and the foreign language you want to learn (maybe Mandarin). There seems no end to the dreams. You tell yourself that you have the time, the energy, the resources, the support – so why not?

But, what really happens? You live each day pretty much as you have been living the days that have recently gone by. You don't go to Easter Island, you do go to California again, and you don't write a book. You write a piece for your writing class and you just keep doing what you've been doing – and to your surprise, you ask yourself, could anything be better?

WHAT'S LEFT?

I guess I started to think about "left overs" the day after Thanksgiving – the turkey is still fresh, the salad is still crunchy, the cranberries still juicy. The pies – they're gone, devoured the day before and everyone is glad because thoughts of all those calories have started to emerge.

But there's a different kind of leftover that fills my mind during this holiday season. My sister Vera and I are "left overs" of the family we grew up in. There were three of us, close siblings and we felt a certain amount of pride that three of us were our family's long-lived survivors.

A few weeks ago, our handsome, charming, caring, 95-year-old brother, died. Now only two of us are left over a large pool of cousins as well, cousins we loved and with whom we shared wonderful experiences.

And, too, we're "left overs" of our generation, often referred to as the greatest generation. Be that as it may, there aren't many left of that generation.

So, what's left? A lot! There are my two boomers, my sister's daughter, several new generations of grandchildren and great-grandchildren, and great nieces and nephews.

I live in a constantly changing world and in the new age of technology; and despite its major problems and crises, it is an exciting world. I have new friends to replace the old and new interests and challenges.

Whatever time is left over for me, it is my time and my challenge – as it has always been – to make the best use of it.

Sunday, March 15, 2009

BACK TO THE FUTURE

There was a letter in my mailbox today from the Alumnae Office of my Alma Mater, Smith College. It announced that this spring would be the 75th Anniversary of the graduation of my Class of 1934. The Alumnae was inviting all members of the class (who were still surviving, I thought) to a three-day reunion on the college campus. All expenses would be covered by the college.

There was one condition: all who attend the reunion were required to be accompanied by another person – spouse (if they were lucky enough to have one in their 90s), a family member, a friend, or an aide. All that person's expenses would be covered too – meals, lodging, entertainment, etc. If a wheelchair, a walker, or a cane were required, that would **not** be on the house!

My mind wandered to 1930, when I entered Smith College. That summer I had celebrated my 16th birthday. The Great Depression was about to have its impact on the world and its inhabitants, as well as college students.

I had never lived away from home, except for summers at sleep away camp. Very few of my friends were going away to college – it was not usual for middle class Jewish girls to leave the protection of their family. I felt like a trailblazer, but I also felt scared. Everything would be so new – Could I manage life on my own? Would I get homesick and want to go home? Would anyone want to be my friend?

I had gone to all girls' high school and Smith College was a girls' college. No reference to girls as women, then. There were no male students, but on weekends there were male visitors on the campus. On other weekends, the campus was deserted as many students left to visit the many male colleges in the area.

Sex was certainly on the minds of some of my housemates. It was a time before the sexual revolution – the time before the birth control pill appeared on the scene, but the diaphragm was not unknown to many of these girls. Its use or misuse did not keep them from worrying about being pregnant. I don't think I ever heard the word abortion.

Although smoking had been common among my high school friends, drinking was not a high school practice then, at least to my knowledge. Some of my friends were not unfamiliar with alcohol. Although it was the era of Prohibition, that did not offer an obstacle. Alcohol was easily available at "speakeasies" in the neighboring towns. I rarely made an appearance there.

The bridge to my acceptance by these girls, a 16-year old Jewish girl from New York, was our mutual interest in learning. Despite their joy in the freedom of their new lives, the opportunity to have fun away from parental eyes, they had a real investment in getting a good education. They accepted the fact that they would probably get married and have children as soon as they found a suitable partner, but they did enjoy the intellectual stimulation provided by the caring and stimulating faculty. Unfortunately, the depression reduced our class to half its size before graduation, but many graduates did eventually pursue careers in their late years.

As I look back on those four years so long ago, I realize that one of the major contributions to my life was that I found my career choice. I majored in psychology, not very popular at that time, but it was during my years at Smith that I began my "love affair" with that field.

All in all, those years so long ago are when I grew up. And now the college is telling me that I need someone to keep an eye on me during my 75th reunion!!

THEN THERE WERE FOUR

Shirley Zussman

Four women traveled to Smith College in the spring of 2009 to attend the 75th Reunion of their Class of 1934. Fit and energetic – no wheel chairs, no walkers, no dementia, yet! Forty-seven other members of the class still survive. All four in their late nineties, the lives of these four women had spanned almost one hundred years. Only a century earlier, women died at an average age of forty-eight. Today the life span of women is close to eighty, so longevity is one of the great gains women have achieved in this century. In the future, it is likely that many more alumnae will attend their 75th Reunion – or event their 100th!

What was life like for the students entering college in the fall of 1930? One thing in common with students today –hard times – the collapse of the Wall Street Stock Market in 1929 had led to the Great Depression – more severe than our recession today.

The immediate impact of the Depression on the Class of 1934 was that a considerable number of students were forced to leave before graduation because of financial problems. When I learned that families tended to keep more of their male (rather than female) children in colleges, I had my first feminist stirrings. Women's education then was considered less important because their goals were chiefly to marry and have children. Of course, many students today have to postpone or interrupt their studies but gender is no longer an issue.

What has also changed is that college women, historically in the minority, now outnumber men in both public and private colleges. Maybe affirmative action for men will be their new battle cry!

Because a large number of women are in the work force today, many in professions, management, and technology positions, their preparation for their future careers started early, often in their undergraduate studies.

The Class of 1934 had a very different focus on their choice of majors, many selecting "The Liberal Arts" – English and French literature, language, music, and drama. I selected Smith – no math required. Today, the entering class at Smith College has some of the same choices as well as different choices – highlighted by the erection of a building devoted to engineering. This preparation for the role in the world of science, government, and medicine is indeed one of the great advances for women in this century.

The four alumnae from so many years ago were asked many questions by current students, who seemed to visualize the Class of 1934 as cloaked in a Victorian mode. Not so!

The Victorian Age ended at the end of the nineteenth century. The Class of 1934 grew up in the Roaring 20s, the Jazz Age, a time of increased social and economic freedom for women, who left their homes for the first time because World War I needed them in factories and offices. The veil of secrecy and repression about sex that had characterized women in the Victorian Era had started to lift, although some remnants of it remain even to this day.

Sexuality was not a subject discussed in the classroom, but it was certainly a subject for discussion in the dormitories. The sexual revolution had not yet occurred and the pill had not yet appeared in the scene, but research indicates that many high school and college students were sexually active during this period. Interest in acquiring more knowledge and, at the same time, learning about themselves led to acquiring whatever books they could on the subject. There were many furies that were trying to keep sexuality covered and repressed.

Sherwood Anderson, Eugene O'Neill, and Ernest Hemingway, wrote books, which contained powerful sexual themes. Students read these with rapt attention they may not have given their assigned readings.

In 1928, Radcliffe Hall, a British author, wrote A well of Loneliness (Banned – Distributed), in which she dealt sympathetically with female homosexuality. Although always whispered about on campus, this book helped to bring this aspect of female sexuality more out from under cover.

Major progress in information about female sexuality came after 1934, with the work of Alfred Kinsey (1955) and later Masters and Johnson. What was firmly established by these researchers was that women's physical and emotional capacity to respond sexually and to find sexual fulfillment was no different than males and even exceeded men's capacity is some respects.

The four women who returned to Smith for their 75th Class Reunion have lived through a remarkable period in the lives of women, a period that opened up a world for them far beyond the domestic dreams they had for their life when they left college in 1934. Like many others in their class, they became part of the changing world. One of the four even became a famous pilot involved in search and rescue operations. Who can predict where the future will take women in the next century?

Technology will continue to change lives, as it already has – even in the sexual realm. There is sex on the internet and there are drugs to enhance experience. Longevity will affect the world of work and the nature of relationships. But as our four returnees look back at the remarkable changes in the lives of women in almost a century since they graduated, they can only hope for even a better world, not only for women, but all of humanity.

95: 'VERY MUCH IN THE MOMENT'

Essay | *By Shirley Dlugasch Zussman '34*

Winter 2009-10 The Smith Alumnae Quarterly

Shirley Dlugasch Zussman '34 is a renowned sex and marital therapist in New York City. She is also the author of numerous articles on relationships. She currently blogs at szussman.blogspot.com.

AN INVITATION CAME last winter from Smith College to attend the 75th Reunion of my class. Images of my college years floated in my mind.

I wanted to be in that time zone again. Never mind that I was 95 years old. I arrived in Northampton in May 2009, eighty years after my first arrival in the fall of 1930. The campus had a dreamlike quality to it.

Joining me were three other members of my class, all of us fit and energetic. No wheelchairs, no walkers, no dementia, yet! Our lives had spanned almost a hundred years - almost as old as this magazine – but we related to one another as if no time had passed. We were very much in the moment. Forty-seven other members of our class are still alive. Only a century ago, American women died at the age of 48. Today, many women, especially in the United States, are starting a new life at that age in a burst of what Margaret Mead called menopausal zest.

Longevity is one of the dramatic changes achieved by women in this century. In the future, it is likely more women will attend their 75th Reunion, even their 100th. More women in this country are going to college today and even outnumber men in both private and public colleges. Another achievement!

How different today's curriculum is than in our time. Today, Smith women are being prepared to take their place in the worlds of engineering, government, medicine, computer science, and economics – wherever their dreams take them. Our curriculum, with its emphasis on literature, music, and art, was shaped to meet the expectation of women to become educated wives and mothers; however, despite the limited career expectations of the class of 1934, many went on to successful careers in many different fields, their early expectations greatly enhanced by women's changing role in society and the opportunities it provided. Julia McWilliams Child, our glorious classmate, provides a perfect example of having started out with a domestic skill and elevating it to a professional and world-famous level.

Our young Reunion guides, thoughtful and curious current students, wanted to know, "What was it like to be here way back then?" They thought of us belonging to the Victorian age. Not so! That age ended at the beginning of the century, followed by the Roaring Twenties, the first emergence of the emancipated woman. World War I had brought women out of the house to work in offices and factories and given them a new freedom. The harsh sexual repression of the Victorian age had begun to subside. It was against this backdrop that the class of 1934, began its college experience, and students relished the new freedom women had. Smoking was common, its dangers still unknown. Drinking was seen as part of the new freedom, even though

Prohibition was the law until 1933.

Our young guides found it hard to believe that some students had sex lives. They knew I was a pioneer in the field of sex therapy – a few of them had read my blog – and wanted to know my ideas about women's sexual feelings and experiences at that time. As I look back, we were not knowledgeable about our sexual selves, about what we needed and wanted. We thought men were the sexual experts and that pleasing our partners was what it was all about. We read books like *Lady Chatterley's Lover* and all of F. Scott Fitzgerald's novels probably more fervently than our assigned reading.

The sexual revolution had yet to come and the pill had not yet appeared on the scene, although diaphragms and condoms were in use. The great contribution to female sexuality came from the works of Alfred Kinsey and Masters and Johnson. These researchers forever eliminated the Victorian concept of women as frigid; they presented scientifically validated evidence that women were equal to men in their capacity for sexual response. They even reported that aging had little effect on female sexuality.

Although we still have much to learn about our sexuality and its role in our lives, as women we are more comfortable today with ourselves as sexual beings, freer to give and receive pleasure.

So here I am writing this piece on my computer – 95 years old – and my journey back in time is over. There have been so many changes, so much we owe to the combined efforts of so many women to enhance our lives, to overcome "the feminine mystique". There will be others in the next 100 years to carry on the mission in a world that even our fantasies cannot construct. But carry on they will!

Despite the limited expectations of the class of 1934, many of us went on to successful careers in different fields.

REFLECTIONS

On the occasion of my 100th birthday party, there was a moment when I looked around deeply aware of my love for the people there and their love for me.

But then I wondered – who are these people that are here? I wondered why parents weren't there; they had delighted in celebrations of all my birthdays. I had pictures to prove it. Where was Jenny, my friend from fifth grade? We spent hours together planning my parties. Where were my camp friends and all those cousins I grew up with, many I did not particularly like, but had no choice to invite to my parties? And where, oh where, was my cherished husband Leon, who I taught to make every occasion a party?

There was no one here from my long-ago past – except my sister Vera, 102 going on 103, and my good friend Ruth, who I have known for 80 years. Of course, I realized quickly – those past dearly beloved were no longer on this earth. I realized how fortunate I was that new friends and relatives replaced them and were here today and how determined I had been to put my grief behind me over my losses and to find new friends and interests. I recalled Shakespeare's lines in his play, <u>As You Like It</u> – "All the world's a stage and men and women merely players. Yes, players come and go but love and devotion seem to endure".

LOST

A few weeks ago my microwave often failed to function and I had to face the fact that I needed a replacement. Shopping in the kitchen department of an electric supermarket, I found a microwave that met my requirements. Looking around the store, I realized that my stove was of ancient origin, too and it seemed practical to buy one while I was in this kitchen heaven.

A few days later, the new equipment arrived. For a brief moment, I had a fantasy that I was the mistress of one of the glamorous kitchens so often displayed in the media. That fantasy soon faded, but I did enjoy the shiny black additions to my kitchen.

Since cooking is not one of my passions and I rarely make succulent roasts in the oven nor any longer bake cookies for my grandchildren, over the years I have stored pots and pans in the lower part of the oven...A I continued to gaze in awe at my new appliances, I suddenly realized that I had failed to remove the pots and pans from my old oven before it was carted away...

Although pots and pans are not inexpensive, it was not the replacement cost that upset me. It was the sudden awareness that I was attached to those old friends. They had played an endearing role in life over the years. One of them went back to my time as a bride. One old pot had seen me through both success and failure as a cook, held many a Thanksgiving turkey and just recently had presented a delicious apricot chicken to a gathering at my home.

And that old frying pan (more fashionably called a sauté pan today) had produced wonderful French toast to many overnight guests before they started to worry about calories. When I told my son about the lost pots, he wistfully asked if the pot that had cooked his favorite childhood food was gone, it wasn't. Many of my pots and pans still remain. They weren't all stored in the oven. But those that are gone seem to have joined with all the other old friends that have disappeared from my life, but leave poignant memories of times past.

ANOTHER RIDE ON A TIME MACHINE II

My son, Marc and I were walking on a New York street on a hot and humid day. Marc commented that we were never on New York streets in the summer when he was growing up. We always spent our summers at our beach house on the Atlantic coast. He said he has never forgotten how much he loved it there.

Suddenly, he said, "let's go there".

A short distance from the city, the next day, we were on the road in my niece's car, the two of them arguing on the best route to take.

As we neared the area, it looked achingly familiar. Soon, we were on our street, in front of our house. We were silent; it didn't look familiar. Why not?

There was a steel gray stucco house. A blanket of glistening green ivy had always covered our house. Its circumference had displayed beautiful blue hydrangeas, blue like the sky. People came from all over the neighborhood to ask how we managed to achieve such beauty in those blossoms.

We walked around to the back of the house. It looked as we remembered it. No tables and chairs to surround a barbecue or to read the Sunday Times. We got involved in political discussions. I even recalled a time when there was a laundry pole where we hung our laundry to dry in the salty air. No dryers then!

I walked behind the garage. There was a grassy space where my daughter and her best friend spent most of their time playing house. I smiled at the memory of them and wiped away a tear. Marc even 'married' this little friend in a mock wedding.

Then, we walked to the beach four houses away. But painfully, we realized it was only three houses away now. Sandy's water fury had washed the house completely away. Marc remembered watching that house built, brick by brick, with his dump truck toy in his hand.

As we walked on the beach, one of the widest among others, we were shocked to see it divided by three sections with steel walls to impede the hurricanes.

But we still loved the sight of the ocean, trying to shut out recent history. Marc plunged in, reveling in the present and remembered pleasure. Age, not the hurricane damage, kept me from joining him.

We didn't meet any friends from the past, but we talked with present residents who we quickly learned also loved the life they led there - the natural beauty, the sense of community, its climate and the constant sound of the breaking surf.

As we began to drive away, there was a faint voice of our beloved housekeeper, Rose, saying, "Why are you guys leaving? I just made a pot roast." Pot roast - a word we shudder at today but was a heavenly treat in those days we couldn't turn back to.

The past and its memories could not nourish us nor appease our hunger, but could only provide a fleeting recall of the days gone by and of who we are today.

MUSINGS ON PSYCHOLOGY

AND SOCIETY

Shirley (left) and Shere Hite (center) at a party in New York City.

TIS THE SEASON TO BE JOLLY

Anticipating a holiday stirs the imagination and offers welcome relief from our everyday worries. Thinking about the Thanksgiving turkey, that special stuffing, the velvety smoothness of the pumpkin pie, makes our mouths water even before the actual meal is placed before us. Hearing the ringing bells, delighting in the twinkling lights, smelling the spicy tang of the Christmas trees lining the streets, evokes the feelings of pleasures to come...

But often, the reality of the celebration doesn't live up to the anticipation. There's fatigue, frustration and disappointment along with the joviality. Anticipation stirs up a fantasy of satisfaction that is often not realized in childhood or in later years.

The idea of going home for the holidays fill sour thoughts weeks before the trip is to start. When we get home there is often the realization that everything has changed or nothing has changed. Amid the pleasure of reunion, there is the memory of past hurts, rivalry, and the dreams that haven't been realized. There is often a feeling of depression about time that can't be relived, the aging clock that can't be stopped.

Where there's no family, few friends, no plans, the loneliness can be more painful than at any other time. And then there's the impact of the world around us. It's Christmas 2008. 'Tis the season to be jolly. We're trying to feel the holiday surge, but have you heard much laughter, seen a lot of smiling faces? Most likely you've heard tales of woe, disbelief about this corrupt and frightening world.

And all that talk about money, money, money. There's an old saying when the Dow goes down the erections go down. Personal relations reflect the tensions and the fears. And then, undercutting our attempts to enjoy the holiday, whatever the circumstances, there is that moment of truth we recall, when we learned there really is no Santa Claus. But then again, there's always the hope that next year he will appear.

MERRY CHRISTMAS AND TO ALL A GOOD YEAR!

THE BEST DAY TREATMENT PROGRAM
IN TOWN IS THE WORKPLACE

You wake up in the morning feeling tired, out of sorts, lonely, wanting only to go back to sleep. Another session with your therapist is not a possibility on this day.

Then you suddenly realize that it's a workday. What a better way to spend the hours ahead that at the office! Better than feeling lonely and sorry for yourself. Better than having nothing to do. There's lots you really need to get done at the office. Best of all, there are people there to greet you, making lunch plans, wanting to include you. You feel a sense of urgency, wanting to get to your work, knowing what you have to do, and do it well.

You take pride in looking good, admiring your image in the mirror when you get dressed – anticipating some compliments. And also, as an extra benefit, you're going to make money if you go to the office. Nobody pays you to go back to sleep.

Some people spend Fridays exclaiming T-G-I-F ("Thank God it's Friday"). But I'm a fan of T-G-I-M ("Thank God it's Monday")!

STALKING THE KIDS

I had been invited to dinner at my nephew's home. When he came to the door to greet me, he said, "Come on in, we're stalking Jennifer". What he meant was that the guests who had already arrived were looking at pictures, hundreds of pictures that Jennifer had sent from Princeton, where she just started a freshman year! There were pictures of her new roommate, the posters on the walls of her dormitory room, of her bed, even her closet. So many pictures! I was quickly tired of them, eager to talk to the other guests, to be in the real world, but the others wanted to see every one of the scenes of Jennifer's new life.

It was not the first time I had wondered about this new and common practice of parents and grandparents and great-grandparents living in the digital world, living vicariously through the lives of their offspring, through pictures on Facebook.

The word my nephew has used – 'stalking' -- seemed suddenly appropriate. I have seen pictures on an iPad of Jennifer at her high school prom. I've seen her low-cut dress and the dresses of her friends. I've seen their breasts almost fully exposed and their bare feet after they've kicked off their high heels. I've seen her prom date. I'm surprised that there wasn't a picture of Jennifer and her date "making out" – I suppose that's yet to come.

Not too long ago, some friends showed me pictures of their children at a sleep-away camp. I saw where they swam, where they ate, where they slept. I saw them pitching in a baseball game and doing a backstroke in the water. I saw them singing around a campfire.

My friends exclaimed how lucky they felt to share these experiences with their children. Lucky? I remember, even though it was so long ago, how lucky I felt going to camp and then away to college – that I was given an opportunity to be on my own, to find out that I could survive without my parents there to help and intervene for me, not even to know about my life away from home. I think the roots of my self-esteem were planted in those days. Then there are the children of my generation – the children of the 60s and 70s, the children of the Free Speech movement and the light cast by "the diamonds in the sky" (The Beatles). They left home to cross the country or to hitchhike in Europe and Asia. There were no cell phones, no long distance calls except in an emergency. Occasionally there was a letter that arrived weeks after it was written. Pictures? If they had a camera, the pictures were developed after they returned home. And they weren't that good!

Today, almost every young person has a good camera, an iPad, a smart phone. This modern technology serves as a bond between parents and children, as does Facebook and Twitter. It serves as a way of keeping in touch as never before.

Does the bond interfere with learning to be independent, to develop one own life style and direction? Who is to say?

Thursday, July 15, 2010

THE FAMILY MEAL

Dinnertime! But where have all the diners gone? Dad called that he's detained at the office. Mom's still at the gym. The teenage boys are at soccer practice. The older sister is studying at her friend's. Even the family dog is still at the animal day care center.

In previous eras, the family meal was almost a sacred table. Mom was still in the kitchen – putting the final touches to a full-course meal. The children knew they had to look neat – their hands washed, their faces scrubbed. No excuses for being late! Whatever subject was being discussed, it was silently acknowledged that father knew best.

With an increasing number of women in the work force, with after-school activities almost mandatory, the chances of the family sitting down together at meal times is markedly reduced. When they are together, often a decision is made to eat out – and there is a whoop of joy – no cooking, no clean up and those French fries at the neighborhood fast food diner!

Is the passing of the family meal something to be mourned? Have we lost an opportunity to transmit family values and to bring together the family to offer support and security? Maybe something is lost, but the family meal wasn't always serene. There were sometimes

113

heated arguments and a feeling of oppression by the woman in charge. And what about boredom – and the wish to get through the meal as quickly as possible and get on with one's own interests?

Of course, families still get together, although surely less frequently around a table. But today, some major change can be observed. With almost no exception, one or both of the children, or even Mom or Dad is on a cell phone, an iPhone or watching a portable video screen. There's more talk to someone not at the family table then there is to someone present. Even couples alone, or a mother and child together, or grandparents visiting from afar, are technologically engaged.

Will the listeners at the other side of the cell phone, the iPhone, or whatever new device is developed – will these connections be the new electronic family? Will the text messages constantly transmitted transmit the cultural values, and offer support and security? The answers lie in the future, a future that will have its own technology, its own questions, and its own search for answers.

NO RING, DON'T BRING

No Ring, Don't Bring may not mean anything to you, but it is a familiar phrase to those involved in the process of planning a wedding, whether they are the bride and groom, their parents or those on the guest list. The ring referred to, of course, is an engagement ring.

The tradition of an engagement ring goes back to ancient times and was popular in many cultures. It has not always meant an agreement to marry, but it often conveyed that promise; it could also be a promise of fidelity, friendship, or eternal commitment. It could be made of metal, stone, or various metals and gems. It is only in modern times that a diamond is the most popular choice for an engagement ring. I guess ever since "diamonds are a girl's best friend" became a popular belief.

The placement of the ring on the woman's fourth finger of her left hand is also a tradition from ancient times based on the belief that there was a vein on that finger that led straight to the heart – the vein of love. There's no reference I found that men have such a vein – so that's maybe why men generally do not wear engagement rings – although they have begun to wear wedding rings.

Today, the engagement ring seems to have taken on a new

function – you might say as a ticket of admission to the wedding – especially for single people. Who is invited and how many guests has probably always been an issue, dependent on many different factors. One issue today is the exorbitant cost of a wedding; therefore, the guest list is carefully surveyed.

Single friends, both male and female, are often told they cannot bring an escort, a date, a dancing partner, or a potential mate unless there is evidence of a committed relationship; and the best evidence of that is the engagement ring! No Ring, Don't Bring!

Tuesday, August 5, 2008

KEEP IN TOUCH

What do we mean when we say, "let's keep in touch?" Why do we talk about being out of touch? What do we mean when we say we were touched by an act of kindness or an expression of sympathy?

I reflected on the word touch as my plane touched ground, my grandson made a touchdown in his school football game, my neighbor told her little girl not to touch the toaster.

There are so many ways in which the word touch is part of our everyday vocabulary. I wanted to touch base to find some thread to connect all these various uses of the word touch. And there it was - it all refers to some kind of connection, some form of contact. Even in utero we are connected with another human being. The first experience we have in life is being touched by another person. Our first exposure to love and pleasure is being held and stroked. Some baby animals die if the mother fails to lick and stroke them. Human babies do not thrive or even survive if they are not touched and held. Toddlers, taking their first steps in exploring the world, run back to their caretakers to refuel, to touch and be touched. Young lovers spend countless hours touching and caressing each other. All the love songs of every generation say "hold me, take me in your arms."

In any modern society, many circumstances require that we keep our distance – don't touch! If strangers brush up against us, even accidentally, we feel frightened. At work, especially in the era of sexual harassment fears, we often act detached, restrained. For most of us, the only opportunity we have to touch and be touched is with our lovers, our mates, our children and their children and even in those situations boundaries exist. Many isolated older people have no opportunity for closeness, for connection, but the hunger for it persists.

Sometimes this hunger finds an outlet in a love affair with a pet, which in turn enjoys the fondling and warm response. Sometimes caring for an invalid or someone else's children helps. Perhaps the popularity of spas is another way contact hunger is met – with massage, manicuring, shampoos – someone focused on your physical self. In a way, cell phones keep us in touch – technology's way to help us connect.

So, keep in touch seems to mean I need to feel connected, I need to touch base with you, perhaps not in the way it used to be in that lost paradise of our earliest connection. It seems we never outgrow our need to touch and be touched.

LET'S KEEP IN TOUCH

Here a phone, there a phone, everywhere a phone, an iPad, a Kindle, a Smart Phone – all highly regarded as a way of keeping in touch with family, business associates, lovers – past and present – and so many friends – thousands of friends on Facebook and Twitter. We're all in touch.

Touching has always been regarded as a basic human need. Babies don't survive if they're not picked up, held and stroked. Animals die if they are not handled and licked.

Previous generations didn't text. They looked into each other's eyes, shook hands, hugged, stroked and caressed each other. Even when they quarreled, there was often physical contact. There's no App for any of that! At least, not yet!

Significant new research suggests that the frequent use of technological devices can be addictive and hard to detach from.

Maybe we'll never outgrow our need to keep in touch digitally, allowing little time to keep in touch in the "old" way, or little desire to do so.

Nor can we predict future ways of being in touch or being intimate. Perhaps fingers will be eradicated. We'll be turned on by touching a screen – already popular with porn. Maybe just as there now are e-cigarettes, there will be e-orgasms. But e-cigarettes are already showing signs of trouble and offer less satisfaction; I wager that will be true of e-orgasms as well if they ever become the "new, new thing".

TECH BABY

About two months ago, I became a great grandmother. Our new family member is a boy, his name is Ariel and he lives in Jerusalem.

My friends congratulated me, commented on how excited I must be and questioned when I planned to visit him. At 95 years of age, the journey to Israel is one I don't contemplate with confidence – so I have decided against it. The possibility of Ariel and his parents coming to New York in the near future is very uncertain.

There are many stories in history and literature of family separation and disbursement, sometimes never to be heard from again. Where there was communication, it was limited and often delayed. But over time, communication improved – the postal system, telegrams and the telephone.

Ariel was born in the era of modern technology. Technology is the way I am getting to know him. I get frequent pictures of him on e-mails and messages about how amazing he is with more pictures. Then, there is Skype, which shows him smiling, moving around, interacting with his parents – and it's free! I can even speculate as to which family member he resembles. He is already a familiar presence on Facebook. If he weren't so young, he would probably be tweeting!

For me, getting to know my great grandson through technology is not very fulfilling. I see babies on screens, in magazines, on the street, and often admire them – but they are not my baby. I personally get pleasure from babies when I can touch them, hold them, taste them, and breathe in their delicious aroma – I can't do that with Ariel.

Maybe in a future era of technology, we can touch them, smell them, cuddle them – but that era has not yet arrived.

CRIME AND PUNISHMENT

I'm sixteen years old, and I am a freshman at Smith College. It is 1930 and they recently built some "modern" dormitories, but I live in an old-fashioned wooden house. It is two-stories high, and I live in a single room on the second floor. I love its old-fashioned charm.

There's a suite of rooms at the end of the hall. It is occupied by seniors who have barely greeted me as we pass each other. But one evening one of them stops me and invited me to join them that evening in their suite. I'm thrilled, to use a phrase popular at that time.

When I arrive at the suite, there are three seniors present. The three of them are smoking cigarettes. Smoking is very popular at that time – its horrors unknown. Smoking is partially forbidden because it is a wooden structure, uninsured, and relatively isolated. Smoking is permitted for one hour after dinner only in the living room.

I've never broken the smoking rule, but I did on that occasion. At about the time I put it out, there is a knock at the door and the "housemother" enters the room. She says that one of the girls has an emergency telephone call – no cell phones at the time and no telephones in the dormitory rooms. She notices the girls who are smoking; my cigarette is finished, and tells them to come to her quarters before breakfast the next morning. They report back to me

123

that they have been given two and two-thirds demerits, one of the most severe punishments before expulsion. They are told that their parents will be notified. I sit quietly and listen.

After they have left the room, I go down to speak to the housemother. I tell her I too had been smoking. We talk and she tells me that since I have told her that fact, I will be given the same punishment and my parents will be notified. She seems reluctant to speak these words. She is obviously upset, but I am calm. Somehow, in the following years, I managed to avoid any more demerits and graduated with my class.

Why am I suddenly remembering this experience so vividly? Why did I take the action I did at that time? What was the motivation? What role has this motivation played in the many years of my life since then?

Monday, September 10, 2012

FORBIDDEN – WHAT MY DAUGHTER SAW IN JERUSALEM

Orthodox Jews are forbidden to watch television, go to the movies or museums where they might see images of naked men and women. Women are forbidden to appear in public without covering their hair or to wear clothing that fails to cover their lower arms, their necks or their knees.

Men are required to wear what we regard as a uniform – a yarmulke or a black hat, black pants, and a white shirt.

There are foods Orthodox Jews cannot eat and books they cannot read. In other words, the secular world in its myriad dimensions is off limits to them.

What my daughter saw as she strolled through Orthodox communities in Jerusalem or joined the huge crowds at the Western Wall were hordes of Orthodox Jews, separate in dress and manner, carrying a prayer book in one hand and in the other hand, the whole of the secular world, their iPhone.

GREEKS

6 – 4th Century B.C.E.

Turning to Ancient **Greece**, it often conjures up, besides its great glories, the subject of homosexuality. There was nothing unique about the existence of homosexuality in Greece. It was practiced and continues to be in almost every period of time and in almost every country. What was different in Greece was that it was fashionable, practiced by the socially elite. Although there were laws against it, it was not kept secret. Wealthy men often attached themselves to young boys who were about 12-20 years old. At the first sign of hair growth on the face the alliance ended. Plato recommended it as a necessary preliminary to a philosophical understanding of a Being. They used the gymnasium (**word gymnos means naked**) where sports were played naked. As evidenced by the greatness of Greek art and sculpture, architecture and language arts, the Greeks worshipped beauty and it included the worship of beautiful adolescent male bodies.

It was a kind of snobbery, very different from the gay pride of today. But an amazing aspect of it was its connection with education. Part of the attachment of the older man was his interest to develop the character of his beloved and to pass on everything he knew to the boy he loved. He was a very dedicated mentor. There was also a conviction that a mysterious affinity existed between physical and moral excellence

126

– and to teach morality was part of the love affair. Since every young man could not have been handsome, the education of the less attractive must have been less passionate and thus less effective. Whether Sappho was a lesbian or not does not rule out that female homosexuality was not unknown.

The Peloponnesian Wars, which practically wiped out the Greek population, changed women's roles somewhat. Remember Lysistrata who told Athenian and Spartan women to deny their husbands intercourse until they signed a peace treaty? Eventually, the society was crushed because barbarians and Romans came from the West and conquered them.

Tuesday, August 26, 2008

AIN'T IT A SHAME!

Shame on you, you should be ashamed of yourself! I am ashamed of you! These are familiar phrases most of us heard sometime in our childhood. Shame is an emotion not often discussed; but, of course, we all know that the Bible tells us that in the beginning there was no shame. According to Genesis, Adam and Eve were both naked and were not ashamed; but, after eating the forbidden fruit, they knew of their nakedness and tried to hide it. Shame thus came into existence.

Since then it's been used in many cultures as a way of teaching children and sometimes adults acceptable behavior. Not unlike Adam and Eve, children are made to feel self-conscious about exposing their bodies or losing control of bodily functions. Feelings of shame and humiliation take root.

There are even shame cultures like Japan after WWII, when their defeat left them with feelings of shame and humiliation. The Muslim culture can be described as a shame culture as well.

As we all know, adults in our culture, at least in recent years, are not made to feel ashamed for exposing large areas of their bodies. The culture does however attribute feelings of shame to the aging body.

128

What a shame – she used to be so pretty! He hasn't got the strength to hit that ball the way he used to. As a society we are very self-conscious about our bodies. We suffer a narcissistic injury when our bodies start to show signs of aging, even as little as a few wrinkles of some gray hairs. Even when we fall ill, some of these feelings emerge. Animals hide when they get sick.

As I've grown older, being self-conscious about my physical self is certainly present, but is it shame I feel? I acknowledge that I "feel ashamed of myself" if I put on weight. Obesity is definitely a state that our culture makes us feel ashamed about.

What I have been aware of is that the need to occasionally ask for help, or be offered a seat on the bus, as it stirs up a feeling of self-consciousness, being yes, slightly ashamed of being perceived as needy.

But there is also the pride of the older person who is active and "doesn't look her age". It prompts me to tell my age, so that I can enjoy the response. "I can't believe it!" You don't look your age", the older person's highest compliment.

Perhaps someday as more people live longer and remain healthy and vigorous, being older will not be accompanied by feelings of self-consciousness, neediness, or shame.

FEELING BLUE

I am in a hotel room in Philadelphia going over some notes in preparation for a talk I am going to give in the morning. Although this is not a new experience for me, suddenly, I feel very sorry for myself to be here alone. It's almost dinnertime. Is it better to order from room service rather than face the embarrassment of requesting a table for one in the good restaurant nearby?

Why do so many of us assume people will look at us alone at a table or buying a single movie ticket and wonder what's wrong with her that she's alone. Doesn't she know anyone who wants to join her?

Men don't seem to be as vulnerable to this situation as women. Maybe because it's assumed that they are alone by choice or business reasons explain it. True, more businesswomen are on the move, but women still seem to feel lonelier in almost any situation on their own.

Where do these feelings of loneliness come from and why are we so reluctant to acknowledge the feeling? Some aspect of it can be traced to the fact that from the moment of conception we are not

alone – we are part of another human being. When we emerge from that dual existence, infants need the care and attention of another human being in order to survive. Long years of nurturing set the pattern for our future need for connection, with friends, lovers, children, and yes, event pets. The first step we ever take is away from our mother, or mother surrogate, with a feeling of joy and excitement, only to quickly return for refueling. In one way or another, it becomes the pattern of our lives – the pull towards independence and autonomy, the need for some refueling, connection, and reassurance that we are not alone. The feat of being without the possibility of connection makes us anxious, which has been referred to by some psychologists as separation anxiety.

For most of us being lonely is a transient state. It makes us sad, uncomfortable or encourages us to find ways to deal with it. For others, loneliness is more intense and is dealt with in ways that become toxic – with food, alcohol, drugs, promiscuity, withdrawal.

Fortunately, there are also positive ways to deal with loneliness. One is to recognize it as part of the human condition. Being alone can offer freedom, self-sufficiency, fantasy, creativity, and time to compose a piece for this class.

BAGGING IT!

Currently, women seem to be obsessed with bags – formerly referred to as pocketbooks, purses, or handbags. Like breasts and buttocks, they come in all sizes and shapes; and like many things in our society, the bigger the better! Some bags are so big that the people carrying them seem dwarfed in comparison and are less noticed then the bag. Why this love affair with bags? They are not the best way to carry around all the many things women seem to need to get through their day. They tie up the hand that is used to carry them; or, if they hang from a shoulder strap, a bag can slip or bump against a woman's body or the body of someone else. Maybe the bump increases the wearer's body awareness of someone else's body. Bags can cause fatigue or backache because of their weight it carried around all day. They can be misplaced or lost or even snatched by a stranger, sometimes in a violent way! They may cause a moment of panic if an object being searched for seems lost in the bag's deep interior.

Men don't have a great way to carry around their needed objects, but they definitely need much less. What they do need, they stuff in their pockets, often having difficulty in remembering which pocket, and often ruining their pants over time. A rare man will sometimes use a bag, only to worry that his sexuality is being questioned. Men seem indifferent to the problem of transporting their stuff, but women seem to love their solution to the problem...

Many bags sell at excessively high prices and thus serve as a status symbol of wealth and fashion know-how. The cost doesn't matter if it serves to have men and women look at this extension of themselves with envy and admiration. But because of manufacturing technology today, women of lesser financial resources can also swing and sway bags almost identical to the original but a fraction of the cost. No matter – real or knock-offs – women love their bags and their ability to draw attention to themselves. Added to their ability to do so, because of their size, it is the rainbow of colors they can choose from in selecting a bag. Black is no longer the color of choice – it's green and red, purple, turquoise, fuchsia, yellow...It's the grown-up delight with all those colorful crayons of childhood! The bag's only rival today is the knapsack, which both men and women use, but it has a utilitarian image. It doesn't swing and sway like breasts and buttocks. It doesn't call out to be noticed; its colors are dull and there is no hint of feminine secrets within. For the most part they are used by younger women; however, the bags know no age limit. Undoubtedly, women will find another way in the future to carry their stuff. But one thing seems likely – there will probably be more stuff to carry proud.

PERSONAL REFLECTIONS

AND TRIBUTES

Shirley as a young lady

Tuesday, August 5, 2008

THE VOICE OF THE SIREN

There are many voices within me that I have listened to in the course of my long life. I can trace them back to my early childhood. Their messages have been loud and clear and I've always listened to them with little resentment or conflict. I've been obedient to their content. "Be a good girl. Be Kind. Be caring. Work hard. Reach for the golden ring on the carousel. Don't envy other because you have so much to be grateful for. Be proud of what you do, what you are".

But there's another voice that has always been there, silent, making no demands, causing no trouble. I guess it never had a chance to be heard against those other voices, so clear, so confident. Lately, that other voice, silent for so long, has begun to murmur, to make its sweet voice audible.

"Come roam the city streets with me and try to catch the tender petal drifting from the trees. Come dance with me. Taste the salt in the ocean waves. Linger in your sensuous bed".

Now, I listen for that voice, let it seduce me, let it lure me down unexplored roads, desire new possibilities. Now, I welcome its siren call!

136

How fortunate I am that that voice is no longer silent and I can enjoy the pleasures it offers me, sometimes in reality, sometimes in fantasy.

REVOLUTION

We met at a party for Loyalist Spain

We talked revolution

Looked at you as a fellow traveler

But then you came to my college town

We walked through the beauty of an early spring

Bursting with tender blossoms, fragrant air

We lay in the lush green grass

We talked revolution

But we felt a new loyalty

I looked at you as a lover

HOW I CELEBRATED MY 58TH BIRTHDAY

We were enjoying a family lunch on a beautiful summer morning. My husband and I, my sister and brother-in-law, and my parents were joined by my brother-in-law's business partner, Ed Hirsh. Ed was what was known in those days as a bachelor, a single man. He was frequent guest at my sister's home and was particularly fond of her eight-year-old daughter. He often talked about the wish to have children of his own.

At some point, I mentioned that I had a birthday the following week. Ed told us, excitedly, that it was his birthday, the very same day. "I'm inviting you all to celebrate next week at my favorite restaurant. They have dance music there and we'll have a wonderful time".

The night of the birthday party arrived and we all met at the restaurant in a festive mood. Ed brought a guest, who I guessed was a professional dancer. The men in the party took turns whirling her around the dance floor.

We enjoyed a wonderful dinner and then a waiter marched to our table with a lighted birthday cake inscribed with my name and Ed's. With a bow to all of us, murmuring "My pleasure" Ed got up to cut the first slice of the cake.

He held the knife high in the air, then suddenly it dropped and Ed fell to the floor. After the first moment of shock, my husband and my father, both physicians, bent down to examine Ed's motionless body. After an interminable moment, they announced that Ed was dead. We all sat there, immobilized, unable to believe that what had just happened was true.

The management of the restaurant called the police and my husband and brother-in-law went with them to identify the body. The rest of us left for home, sad and silent.

Early the next morning, there was a telephone call for my husband, a very frequent occurrence in our household. This time it was not a patient. A woman identified herself as the wife of the man who had died in the restaurant last night, the man known to us as Ed Hirsch and to her as Tom Gilbert. The morning pages had written up the story of the way Ed had died and my husband's name was mentioned in the article as the physician who had been present. The woman described that their family lived in Queens and that she and their two daughters had been expecting Tom to be home last evening and had prepared a surprise birthday for him. She knew his work as a traveling salesman and said he was often on the road. She was completely unaware that he was a partner in a prosperous business.

There were many complex developments to this story, but that's another story. This is the story of how I celebrated my 58th birthday.

AMERICAN AIRLINES, FLIGHT 15, MAY 16, 2008

A few months ago, I boarded an American Airlines flight to San Francisco. As I settled down in my seat it was announced that boarding was almost complete. At the last moment someone sat down in the empty seat next to me. He was dressed in the garb of an Orthodox Jew – white shirt, black pants, yarmulke and he had a long beard. His beard, unlike many other Orthodox Jews I have observed, was not white, but dark brown. Obviously, this was because he was a young man.

When we were in the air, I turned to him and said, "It's Bashert that I am sitting next to you". Bashert is a word I often use to mean fated or destined. It is one of the few words in my Yiddish vocabulary.

My seatmate turned to me with a smile and said, "Bashert is usually used to convey a mating situation and I don't think you have that in mind".

We shared a laugh and then I told him what I did have in mind. My grandson, a graduate of the University of California, a 6'4" surfer, had joined a Yeshiva program in Israel and had become an Orthodox Jew. My family members, none of whom were observant Jews, were all disturbed by this situation. When I referred to my grandson as Chris, my seatmate, who told me his name was Menachim, said he got the picture.

Menachim and I made a remarkable connection during the rest of our flight to San Francisco. We laughed, we talked, and we shared the food we had brought along. I paid attention when he prayed and he listened to my concerns. Nothing changed in the way I thought about the situation, but something changed in my tolerance of it.

He e-mailed me several times to inquire about how I had enjoyed my trip and then came an e-mail, "How are you with Passover, Shirley, we would be very happy to have you join our family for the Seder we are having in Brooklyn". I didn't accept the invitation, but it warmed my heart.

A few weeks after, my grandson was visiting me in New York on his way to Israel after a visit with his parents. Menachim, his wife, Chris and I had lunch together. He came in his Orthodox garb, this time with a large black hat, which I've always??? His wife, a pretty woman, with blonde hair, which I later realized must be a wig, was fashionably dressed and I would not have identified her as Orthodox. She was interested and involved with us. Both she and Menachim had their blackberries on the table and received a number of calls. He told us he was leaving for Paris later that day.

What is my attraction to this man? He is charming, humorous, warm and is very present. He is a man of considerable energy, involved with his family, friends, synagogue and an active real estate developer in Israel, Russia and the Ukraine.

I think across the barriers of age, religion, background and worldviews, we genuinely like each other. But do I have a hidden agenda in involving myself in this relationship? I think so. In my fantasy, I think it's Bashert that in some way he's going to rescue my grandson.

As he was at the door, almost to leave, I turned to Menachim and said, "If it weren't against your tradition, I'd love to give you a hug".

The next morning Menachim called me. He said he had told his wife about my wanting to hug him. Her response was, "You should have let her. She's an old lady".

NEVER TOO LATE

I first met Vivian in an exercise class. I was impressed with her energy, her air of confidence, and a quiet presence I thought of as dignity.

I made some friendly overtures to her, chatting before class started and suggesting we go to coffee sometime; but it was clear Vivian was not interested in our getting together. She always left with her friend Alice, a long-time friend.

Vivian left exercise class long before I did. I was surprised when our paths crossed in a book club we had both joined. Vivian had an extraordinary knowledge of modern and classical literature – which we all appreciated.

Vivian was much more a member of the book club group that she had been in the exercise class. I attributed it to the fact that, without Alice, she was much freer to interact with all of us.

Eventually, Vivian and I became friends – as close as some of the friends in my past. How was that possible, I asked myself? We didn't grow up together; we weren't in the same class in kindergarten, or high school, or college. We never pledged to be (BFF) best friends forever.

Vivian didn't know my story, my parents, and she didn't dance at my wedding. We weren't professional colleagues. She never met my husband – nor I hers. She never shared the intimate secrets of my life's various stages.

How, then, could I regard her as a close friend – but I did. We knew each other's older selves and we shared what it meant to grow old.

VERA – 102 GOING ON 103

Yesterday was my sister Vera's 102nd birthday. If you have an image of an old, infirm woman barely able to participate in any birthday celebration, discard that image! Instead, see her walking down the street in her patterned stockings, her beautiful jacket, and her makeup perfect. It's not rare for some to ask, where do you get you haircut or where can I find that raincoat?

Vera never complains of any aches or pains. I can't remember a time when she was sick. She foolishly, according to my opinion, never had a mammogram or pap test in her earlier years. Now, she does get flu shots and has an annual physical exam.

When I telephone and ask, as I might anyone, how are you, she always answers fine, as if what a foolish question, how can I be anything but fine?

Reaching 102 doesn't mean what it might mean to most people. She says it is only numbers to her. She states quite firmly that she's not any older because of the numbers. She doesn't feel any older than she felt many years earlier in her life. As a psychologist, I think to myself – it's a state of denial – but then I just wonder maybe it's the way aging is for her.

No sign of dementia for her either. She is very alert, very much in the present, no preoccupation with past memories for her. She still has passionate interests in politics, Obama, reading, fine restaurants – although she eats very little – both to remain very trim (it's in) and she believes in a healthy diet. She never takes a drink, although in former years she enjoyed wine with her meals.

Vera often tells me one advantage of a long life is that you can see the story unfold. She's interested in the unfolding of world events, very interested even more so in the unfolding of her family's story. She does not boast about her family as so many people do; she doesn't need to, as other people exclaim what a remarkable family she has.

Vera has one daughter Linda and Linda has three sons, who are Vera's grandchildren; and they in turn among them have 7 children, who are Vera's great grandchildren, who range in age from 6 to 19. They were all gathered together to celebrate her birthday. They are extremely attractive, charming, and great fun. But above all, was the atmosphere of love for Vera and for each other.

What is also remarkable about this family is that the three grandchildren, ranging in age from 40 to 50, seem to have achieved outstanding success in the financial world – all three – (no black sheep here) and they are close brothers, living very near to each other, with wives seemingly cut from the same cookie cutter, each of them has their own successful careers and the three couples are almost a little community – although they branch out with their friends and special interests.

Happy Birthday Vera

102 Going on 103

You have some kind of key

But the years fly on so fast

Baby, keep having a blast!

SPENCER

Born at the end of World War I, at last Sara and Louis had a son. Shirley and Vera had a brother. A special one, like no other, swiftly, swiftly flew the years. Filled with laughter and with tears. Student, camper, sailor, – and more.

He even answered his country's call to war. Then years of a busy working life and Spencer found himself a wife. Husband, father, grand and great grandfather too.

A more loving, caring man than most of us knew.

And then came Loretta, could anything have been better!

HAPPY BIRTHDAY MARC

Not being with you today brings on my tears.

But hey, we have been together for a lot of years.

So, here from New York, I'm wishing you well.

And from your past I have a few stories to tell.

You were born in 1946 at the end of World War II along with 74 million others like you.

It was a "baby boom" and you were among the first to be labeled a "boomer".

A Cesarean delivery is how you came into the world. It is speculated by some that such a procedure has an emotional effect on the baby. If there is some truth to that you certainly won that one.

You were a lively, joyful child. We used to call you "laughing boy".

After your sister Carol was born, you had a built-in friend. And that still holds.

Friendship has always been and still is a great source of pleasure for you. You chose it as your major, but somehow you managed to get your homework done.

The Berkeley days changed your life. Your first call home was to reassure us you weren't in jail. The Free Speech movement started to roar.

But you are at a party not reading a book, there is more to tell – becoming a husband and father to Rayna and Michael, my adored grandchildren. And Becky, your wonderful wife – the light of your life; and what about Austin, how lucky can you get.

As I have always told you some many times, Marc, you squeeze the juice out of life.

Now there is Jonah, almost two, the son of Michael and Alana, his wonderful wife.

Your path to your career is another story to tell – but yours to tell.

You're still a boomer and have been one along the way – but with the birth of Jonah, your little grandson, you are running now with the grandfather boomers – enjoy the trip!

A LETTER TO MY DAUGHTER CAROL

Full of charm and grace, and, oh my God, what a beautiful face. (I'm a rhymer. Some things do endure.) From early on, you longed to roam, explore the world and—to my lament—only touch base with home. Your audacious interests attracted friends who joined with you in following current trends. I stood on the sidelines and marveled.

Raised in the sixties, you were immersed in the youth movement that changed the culture of the time. It influenced the person you became. It inspired your values and world view, along with your taste in music, dance and dress style. I tried to keep up though I was probably just running in place.

From early on, you had an interest in spirituality as a way of helping you to understand the world, your inner self, and what was important to you. From whence this came remains a mystery, though I must say these foreign ideas put my Freudian perspective to a hint of a test.

Born, bred and educated in New York City, you began to yearn for the beauty of nature and relief from the noise and stress of city life. Like many of your generation, you yearned for greener pastures. As a byproduct, you made me reaffirm that I thrive on the urban pulse.

Your interest in exploring the world motivated you to go west to Taos, then California. There you found natural beauty, a social conscience, and deeper spirituality with an emphasis on a life of change. There you discovered living in the present. There you found soul-touching natural beauty and the freedom of living by experimentation. There you found a career choice and trained to become a marriage and family therapist, a calling you still pursue today. So in the end you are truly and joyfully your mother's daughter for staying in the family business!

In California, you met Climbing Sun (yes, that's his name) who became your lover, your husband, and your lifetime partner in work and play. And the balance must be emphasized: *so* much work, *so* much play!

In California, you raised a son, Yair—now the father of your grandchildren. Never one to stagnate, you moved to Florida to be near Yair and your grandchildren. And closer to me as well. It's almost as if it were planned.

Carol, from the very start, you have filled my heart with joy and pleasure—sure a few conflicts along the way. I prefer to see them as spices added to the stew of our lovely relationship—and your elegantly lived life.

Thank you for being who you are then and now!

Your Mom

RECIPE FOR A HAPPY MARRIAGE

Ingredients

2 people reasonably sound in mind and body.

3 large cups of getting to know each other before tying the
 knot.

1 large tbsp. of learning about each other's faults and virtues.

Several measuring spoons of accepting that you can't change
another person; it's hard enough to change oneself.

12 oz. of agreement that you each have – separate interests
you want to pursue and some degree of space required that
you need to regulate.

Pour in a large bottle of luck, mazel, good fortune, and
prayers to whatever God may help you.

Sprinkle the mixture with whatever spices you each like and
start stirring in one of those bowls you received from your

gift registry. Keep stirring until the mixture is smooth and relatively free of lumps. There are always some lumps and bumps in every couple pairing.

Your oven should have been preheated in the time you were getting to know each other – now turn it on high and put your dish into a hot oven and keep it hot.

Because Alana and Michael have all the ingredients for his recipe and they are both good cooks, I predict a successful outcome for this recipe – which I hope they'll enjoy for many, many years to come.

Biography

Shirley Dlugasch Zussman was born on July 23, 1914, five days before the beginning of World War I. She was born on the Lower East Side of Manhattan to Dr. Louis Dlugasch, a physician, and Sara Steiner, a surgical nurse. Her family soon moved to Brooklyn where Shirley lived until graduating high school.

Shirley attended Smith College and graduated in 1934. Soon after, she attended the Columbia School of Social Work, and then embarked on her career that took her to such places as the Jewish Family Service, the Child Development Center of the Jewish Board of Guardians, and Lenox Hill Hospital Psychiatric Clinic.

She married Dr. Leon Zussman, an Obstetrician-Gynecologist, in 1940, with whom she had two children, Marc and Carol. She began doing more psychotherapy in private practice, and earned her doctorate in 1957 at Columbia University Teachers College under the personal tutelage of Dr. Margaret Mead.

In 1966, Shirley and her husband began to work with the celebrated sex therapists William Masters and Virginia Johnson. As a dual sex therapy team, the Zussmans were co-directors for ten years at the Human Sexuality Program at Long Island Jewish Hillside Medical Center. Shirley and Leon lectured around the world, wrote many articles, and were featured on TV and radio. Together they wrote *Getting Together: A Guide to Sexual Enrichment for Couples* (William Morrow, 1979). After her husband's death in 1980, Shirley was elected twice as President of the American Association of Sex Educators,

Counselors and Therapists. She wrote the monthly column "Sex and Health" for Glamour Magazine for fifteen years, and "Talking Sex" for a children's magazine. She has been a guest on Donahue, Twenty/Twenty, the NBC Nightly News, CBS News, Oprah, and Barbara Walters. Shirley has been sought for interviews by many major publications including New York Magazine, Cosmopolitan, USA Today, Mademoiselle, Harper's Bazaar, Vogue, Newsweek, New York Post, and New York Times.

Amazingly, Shirley has continued her private practice, lecturing and writing, up through to the present time at 103 years old. The writings in this book are drawn from her blog "What's Age Got to Do With It," started in her nineties, and other even more recent writings.

She is presently participating in a weekly writing group, which she considers the highlight of her week. Shirley lives on her own on the Upper East Side of Manhattan. She is actively involved as a mother, grandmother, great-grandmother, family member and dear friend to many others.

Made in the USA
Coppell, TX
20 December 2021

69763717R00089